D0515201

Descending
★ the Dragon

• •

MY JOURNEY DOWN THE COAST OF VIETNAM

JON BOWERMASTER

My initial request to bring kayaks to Vietnam had
been greeted by the government man who controls
visits by journalists with five simple words:
"That will be quite impossible."

▣ NATIONAL GEOGRAPHIC

WASHINGTON, D.C.

Published by the National Geographic Society
1145 17th Street, N.W., Washington, DC 20036-4688

Copyright © 2008 National Geographic Society
Text copyright © Jon Bowermaster
Photographs copyright © Rob Howard

All rights reserved. No part of this book may be reproduced or transmitted in any form or by any means, electronic or mechanical, including photocopying, without permission in writing from the National Geographic Society.

ISBN: 978-1-4262-0304-6

Library of Congress Cataloging-in-Publication Data available upon request.

Founded in 1888, the National Geographic Society is one of the largest nonprofit scientific and educational organizations in the world. It reaches more than 285 million people world-wide each month through its official journal, NATIONAL GEOGRAPHIC, and its four other magazines; the National Geographic Channel; television documentaries; radio programs; films; books; videos and DVDs; maps; and interactive media. National Geographic has funded more than 8,000 scientific research projects and supports an education program combating geographic illiteracy.

For more information, please call 1-800-NGS LINE (647-5463) or write to the following address: National Geographic Society, 1145 17th Street N.W., Washington, D.C. 20036-4688 U.S.A.

Visit us online at: www.nationalgeographic.com/books

Interior design by David Skolkin / Skolkin + Chickey, Santa Fe, NM
Printed in Singapore

Page 1: Evening delivery on an unusually quiet Hanoi street
Page 2–3: Exploring the Ben Hai River, once the dividing line between North and South Vietnam

Contents

Introduction

· ·

★ VIETNAM'S HISTORY IS constructed atop the myths of dragons. Its capital was once known as the City of Dragons; its kings, for centuries, tattooed themselves with dragon imagery. Its people believe they originated from a union between a dragon and a fairy. As the myth goes, the dragon came from the sea, the fairy from the mountains. Betrothed, they gave birth to a hundred sons. When the dragon grew tired of living far from his beloved sea and returned to it, fifty sons followed. Today people up and down the narrow country still believe they are descended from one or the other, the dragon or the fairy.

It was the love of the sea that sets the dragons of Vietnamese myth apart from all others. The Vietnamese dragons were known to live on and under the sea, as deep as ten thousand feet below the surface, hidden from all but the wiliest of predators. These undersea creatures would hide themselves in the deep waters where they would grow fins and horns and change shape and size at will. One day, after taming the ocean's currents, one such creature stepped so heavily on the earth that deep valleys were formed, which quickly filled with water when the beast plunged back to sea. The peaks of the mountains left behind formed a multitude of rocky islands, and the bay was renamed Ha Long—"where the dragon descends to the sea."

Find a map. Put your finger on Vietnam and trace its eastern edge, its seventeen-hundred-mile frontier. It truly is shaped like a ridged

The constant toot of motorcycle horns forms the soundtrack of today's Vietnam.

dragon's back. I have been tracing that outline for many years, on a half-dozen different trips between 2000 and 2007, spending months at a time moving slowly down the coast from the border of China through Hanoi, the Imperial City of Hue and south to Hoi An. My primary interest has always been the north. Given the region's prominent role in recent history as home to "the enemy," and as a place I felt few foreigners, especially Americans, understood or knew, I have focused my travels there to try to give its people a voice beyond the cliché. What has always surprised me in a country with so long a reputation for war is that today's Vietnam is filled with gentle, peaceful people.

Usually I prefer traveling alone, or with one companion. My most intense travel along the coast was in 2001. During that trip a team of four and a handful of monitors, drivers, and hangers-on accompanied me for two months. The stories that follow are drawn from all my travels, but particularly from that trip.

Prologue

● ●

★ WOKEN THIS MORNING by a symphony of Hanoi street sounds rushing in over my balcony... the first bleats of the army of motos that propel the city, the gentle cry of a local Jimi Hendrix soaring out of an alley near Hoan Kiem Lake, the scrape of metal grates being pulled back from storefronts, the crow of an urban cock. My room in the Dan Chu ("Democracy") Hotel is in the center of Hanoi. I open the wooden window shades and peer down onto the street. A mother and daughter bicycle past, a scooter repairman is already at work, sipping a morning tea. Hundreds of sagging and twisted telephone and electric lines crisscross above the streets. The air is humid, made heavier by the mixed-up smell of streetside-made soup and diesel exhaust. Good morning, Vietnam! Before the sun has fully risen, I'm on the sidewalk.

Quickly the air has filled with the primary din of big-city Vietnam, the cacophony of tooting horns from the swarms of motos, bicycles, buses, and occasional private cars that crowd the wide streets. There are now 2 million motor scooters alone in Hanoi (in a city of 4 million), a thousand registered anew every day. "They are our legs," says my friend Qiang. The real thing—Honda Dreams, made in Japan—can cost more than two thousand dollars; the imitations from China, called Waves and Loves, go for seven to eight hundred dollars. All are expensive in a country where big-city earners bring home four hundred dollars a year, their rural counterparts not much more than two hundred. Girlfriends in silk dresses ride sidesaddle, grasping onto young boys' waists with one arm while simultaneously talking into mobile phones. Old men wear army helmets, the younger let their hair blow free on imitation Harleys (a new mandatory helmet law is the most controversial subject in the country). Everything is transported by scooter, from bamboo baskets of chickens to plate glass windows, kegs of beer to fat pigs.

I stop for a breakfast of hot soup served out of a black pot boiled on a street corner by a rudimentary gas stove. The old mama drops pieces of raw fish into the roiling broth and hands me a plastic bowl. She offers me a snake from a jar, to be added to my soup. I pass. Squeezing into one of the plastic kiddy chairs that the Vietnamese have no problem fitting into, my knees ache as I slurp. We are sitting in front of a store that sells only ladders. Every shop on this narrow street in the Old Quarter sells only ladders. One street over, they sell only funeral wreaths. Parallel and perpendicular streets specialize too: plumbing fixtures, plastic kitchenware, shoes, furniture, brooms, clocks, silk. On the curb a man in his seventies pounds a crumpled piece of aluminum with a stone tool, trying to shape a repair for his moto's exhaust. Behind most storefronts are sweatshops; walk the streets and peer down the alleys and it's easy to catch a glimpse through an open door of workers hunched over badly lit tables, making everything from silk scarves to plastic sandals.

On the shore of Hoan Kiem Lake an elegant man in blue-and-white striped pajamas, silver-framed glasses, and slippers practices tai chi, either not noticing or not caring that he's no longer in his bedroom. He's joined by a man with his yellow-white hair pulled back in a neat ponytail, a red rose tied into the knot. Gaggles of men gather around games of checkers played on boards drawn onto the cement, shouting encouragement, coaching, cheering. Many of them are missing limbs.

Near the Opera House, sun now glinting off its high windows, haircutters litter the sidewalk with strands of long, thin, black hair. Their mirrors hang from hooks on sheets of corrugated metal or utility poles. Doctors and dentists perform checkups and small procedures on the sidewalk, long lines of women patiently waiting in tiny red-and-blue plastic chairs. Women in conical hats and betel-stained teeth carry scales under one arm and heavily loaded baskets of oranges, mung beans, and seaweed-wrapped pork under the other. Market windows advertise roasted dog, sheathed eggs cooked in coals, beans of every type; there is an overpowering smell of grilling and open sewers. The biggest street corner business? Bicycle tire pumping.

Past the elegant Metropole Hotel competitive badminton matches are played on an asphalt triangle squeezed between lanes of traffic. Cyclo boys sleep beneath the shade of sycamore trees. Before taking a seat on a nearby bench, an old man pulls a paper napkin from the pocket of his navy blue cotton pants and carefully wipes it clean of dust. Bailing wire and string hold his bicycle together. Insistent—but not overly insistent—boys offer shoe shines or badly photocopied black-and-white postcards and copies of the *Quiet American* and *The Sorrow of War*. They have a multitude of potential sales targets; the streets squaring the lake are filled with tourist buses offloading aged visitors (among the 4 million who now come to Vietnam each year), many of them whose first stop in Hanoi is the water puppet theater.

I'd been in Hanoi several times already, subtly attempting to twist the arm of the government to approve my planned exploration of Vietnam's coast by sea kayak. While charmed by the early morning urban scenes, my target is the seventeen-hundred-mile coastline of Vietnam. I am ready to be on the sea, the South China Sea.

My goal is straightforward: To kayak the coastline from near Mong Cai on the China border to Hoi An, just south of Da Nang, covering about eight hundred miles. The adventure would take about two months. One reason the government is balking is because no one has ever asked permission for such before. It is understandably concerned about my team's safety and wonder about our ability to take care of ourselves on the open sea. The headline they most fear would read something like "Five Americans Drown Off Coast of Vietnam." They are also worried that our route might compromise certain "military sensitivities" as we descend the coastline, a concern that confounds me since we are just five traveling by plastic kayak. So far my requests had been answered by no's. "Unprecedented, unnecessary, unsafe, unwise," was the official response.

I have been drawn to Vietnam by just how little I know about life here post-1975, when what the Vietnamese still call the American War ended. I am curious about the geography, the land, and the environment of the narrow nation, and we will see a wide cross section, from the

thirty-five hundred limestone islands of Ha Long Bay to jungles running right down to the sea and then the wide sandy beaches that run for hundreds of miles south from Da Nang.

But mostly I want to meet its people. One-third of Vietnam's 85 million live on or near the coastline, making their livelihoods off the sea. We will be traveling primarily in what was North Vietnam; until roughly 9/11/2001 the people we'd be meeting were our last great enemy, clad in black pajamas rather than turbans, hiding in swamps not caves. Time has passed, much around the world changed, and the people of Vietnam—unlike many Americans—are long past the war, having moved on to the more important daily effort of simply making a better life for themselves. Prosperity hardly followed peace and one result is that Vietnam is still an extremely poor country, one of the most impoverished in Southeast Asia. I am relentlessly curious to hear their stories and see how they react to us.

The kayaks will allow us to approach from the sea, get us to places we could not reach by land, and maybe connect us to the people in a way different than if we had arrived overland, hopefully more as equals than

as visitors. Our seventeen-foot-long plastic boats will serve as floating ambassadors in a country where just thirty years before we would have been seen as targets rather than friends.

One-third of Vietnam's 85 million people live along the coast and depend on the sea for jobs and food.

I am also curious to see how this place might change me. These are my first visits to Vietnam. I turned eighteen in 1972, the final year that a lottery picked new American soldiers. My lottery number was high—278—but there was little chance of my being drafted anyway, since by then the war was largely discredited, politicians on both sides desperate to find a way out. The images I had of Vietnam came from books and television and movies and revolve around war; I am anxious to see how the country has evolved in the twenty-five years since its end.

My partner in this adventure couldn't have had a more different life experience. Having escaped from Saigon by helicopter on the last day of the war in 1975, Ngan Nguyen was three years old when she arrived in the United States. Though she mostly grew up in New Orleans, which helped shape her worldview, she is still very much Vietnamese; almost thirty years old, she shares many of the same curiosities as I do about the north. She's returned to Vietnam many times, as a student and then aid worker, employed by UNICEF and then OXFAM. But she barely knows the north. Her discoveries as we explore the coastline together—about herself, her country, her countrymen, and her place in both cultures—will inevitably open new wounds daily, even as others heal.

At night in Hanoi I seek out anyone who might teach me about modern-day Vietnam. Professors, journalists, politicians, veterans of war, young office workers, the occasional drunk in a bar. One night at dinner at the Red Onion, an elegant restaurant next to a former POW prison, around the table are a Nike marketing manager, a returned Vietnamese (collectively known as Viet Khieu) who had grown up in Seattle and now owns coffee plantations in the highlands, the outgoing bureau chief of the *Los Angeles Times* and his filmmaker wife, a four-foot-ten Vietnamese madame, and the right hand to the then ambassador to Vietnam from the United States. Much of the conversation revolves around the "nature" of the typical Vietnamese.

The coffee man had only recently moved to Ho Chi Minh City (Saigon) from Hanoi and he found the pace here preferable. "I used to be bored with how long it takes to get anything done here. I remember my most often repeated phrase on the streets of Hanoi was 'C'mon old man, hurry up, let's get on with it,' whether it was a store clerk or someone walking on the street. But now I appreciate the slower pace. What's the hurry after all?"

"They may seem slow but they are among the most determined people on the planet," says the man from the State Department. "How else to explain why the Vietnamese, who've been at war most of the past one thousand years, were able to beat back just in the past fifty years the Japanese, the French, the United States, plus incursions from Cambodia and China?" He analogizes Vietnamese today to flies in a closed jar, beating their wings furiously to gain a freedom that still seems far off. The average wage for a Vietnamese worker today is $211 a year—far less than even its similarly impoverished neighbors in India and China.

Each has a mixed view of Vietnam's immediate future. The American filmmaker tells me, "They are just waiting for the yoke (of oppression) to be lifted. Then you'll see this place change overnight. Vietnam is communist in name only. Things have changed so much in the past five years; wait another five before you judge it."

The man from State disagrees. "Real change here is a long way off. These are desperate, despairing people—especially anyone older than thirty. My advice? Watch China. As China changes, so will Vietnam."

The Nike man offers an employer's view. "They are not a very effective people. They are so used to being poor that they do a half-ass job . . . because that's all they can afford.

"For example, say they've got a chair with a broken leg. They will pick up some bent nails from the street, straighten them, and put the chair back together . . . even though they know it won't last more than a day or two. And then they'll have to fix it again in the same manner. It's a small example, but on a bigger screen that's why foreign investment—especially American—hasn't been as forthcoming as expected. The four top foreign investors are all Asian—Japan, Korea, Taiwan, China, and then comes the U.S. I think that's because the Asian countries understand the Vietnamese way of doing things, which includes extra patience and never getting angry, which doesn't accomplish anything here. Get angry and they ignore you. Completely."

Investor or journalist, entrepreneur or adventurer, communist or capitalist, what is it that attracts us to this place not so far removed from war, a country where the prime north–south artery, Highway 1A, is still pocked with bomb craters and the victors still suffer one of the world's worst poverties?

Morbid curiosity? Many come to see the sites of famous battles where vendors peddle dog tags, bullets, and coins dug from the blood-stained soil.

Coming to grips with having lost? There are public logs at some of the most famous battle sites, like Khe Sanh, in which returning American soldiers have scribbled regrets, pride, and lasting confusion.

The booming tourism business here—more than 4 million foreign visitors a year—makes me wonder how long it will be before soft adventure cravers are allowed into Iraq to wait in lines to visit Saddam's palaces and al Qaeda's caves. Maybe even one day to visit a mausoleum featuring the slightly green, embalmed body of Osama bin Laden. Ho Chi Minh and his elaborate cement version draws large crowds daily to the heart of the capital city. For many years Hanoi symbolized hate and repression; I wonder, will Westerners again travel safely to Baghdad for holiday?

Make no mistake. Despite the tourist boom and burgeoning free market economy, Vietnam is no Thailand. It is not yet a place for back-packers or rave-seekers, not high on the list for sex tourists or wife-seek-ers. The government in Hanoi has little patience with the kinds of freedoms we take for granted, like speech, religion, press. E-mails are monitored, outspoken religious leaders jailed without charge, anyone speaking or writing ill of the government goes immediately, sans trial, to jail. As a visitor you get a thirty-day visa, that's it. No lingering, no hang-ing out, no second homes on those wide sandy beaches.

My asking began in an office in a rundown, dirty-yellow French colonial building in Hanoi, headquarters of the government's Foreign Press Cen-ter (FPC), one year before I planned to return with kayaks and a team. A pair of lazy guards lounged at the gated entrance and waved me in.

Luong Than Nghi, the FPC's deputy director, welcomed me to his office in the back of the building. I needed his permission to come to Vietnam, as does any foreign journalist, and had been faxing and Fedex-ing him for months—maps, proposals, guarantees, anything he asked for, anything I could think of to salve what I knew was a government still suspicious of journalists, especially Westerners. All of my missives sat in a heap on his desk. I understood from the onset that our exploration would come with certain handcuffs. Not just the twenty-four-hour-a-day monitor who would follow us every step, but also firm dictates about where we could and could not go, who we could and could not speak with. The video we would shoot for a National Geographic documentary film would have to be screened—censored—by the FPC before we would be allowed to leave the country. Either I agree to those terms, or we would not be allowed. I was desperate to come, so will-ing to negotiate.

With his encouragement, I explained again what I hoped to do: Sea kayak from the border of China through Ha Long Bay to Hoi An, roughly eight hundred miles. A team of five, making reportage and film for National Geographic, mostly curious about the people we'll meet who live and depend on the sea.

He listened, sucking heavily on a Marlboro Light, which was turning the closed-up room hazy with cigarette smoke. Smiling, he looked up through the fog.

"Mr. Jon, thank you for coming. I understand what you want to do. I appreciate it very much.

"But that will be quite impossible. . . "

One year later I find myself in the same building, same room. It is my first meeting with Duong Linh, the Foreign Press Center monitor who has been assigned to accompany us 24/7 during our two-month exploration. Ultimately I convinced them to allow us in and had shipped kayaks over from South Carolina that had arrived two months before. The deal-maker? Cold hard cash, which they were billing as a "filming permit." I bring thick envelopes filled with eight thousand dollars, which I will hand over to Linh on predetermined dates during the two months. I never ask about its final destination.

Linh and I sat in the great room at the front of the house. One of twenty censors working out of the Hanoi office, his most recent assignment with Westerners was with the Travel Channel, filming a series on Vietnamese restaurants. "I gained ten kilos on that one," he smiled, admitting it was a "great" assignment. Every time a foreign journalist applies to visit Vietnam, if approved, they are assigned a monitor and accompanied. Everywhere.

We'd been corresponding for nearly a year and I'd asked around about him and his reputation. He's admitted he's not big on the water, or swimming, which should make our travel together interesting since we'll be spending most of our days on the ocean. What we have planned won't be particularly arduous physically, nor treacherous as long as we avoid pirates and the occasional typhoon, but it is a first. While the government has allowed kayakers in the most touristed spots—Ha Long Bay in the north, Nha Trang in the south—they have never before authorized kayaking along the central coast. "Military sensitivities" remains the mantra, which we would hear over and over.

I'd had lunch the day before with a wire service reporter based in Hanoi, a returning Viet Khieu, and she expressed surprise that they had granted us visas, especially during this time. "It's right when the Ninth Party Congress is meeting, in which the Communist Party lays out its 'vision'—which we know they don't have!—for the next five years. Normally during those meetings they try and keep all foreign journalists out of the country, in case there is some kind of demonstration or street protest. That they have allowed you in suggests they are loosening up or somehow convinced you are not a threat."

Dressed in a light blue suit, blue shirt, and gray paisley tie, his socks robin egg blue to match, his jet-black hair just cut, Linh's most identifying style mark are his inch-long thumbnails. They are evidence to anyone in the know that this is a man of leisure, not the working class. Twenty-eight and well educated, he admits during our first meeting that he doesn't care if I represent National Geographic or the *Hoboken News*. "Basically, I see all journalists from the West as bad news. An unnecessary risk. But I'm here to help you, make sure you have a safe and productive journey."

Ultimately he is in the control business. Control to the extent that before we leave Vietnam two months from now all of the video we have shot, probably more than forty hours' worth, will be returned to this office and screened by him and his associates. He's personally invested in our storytelling. If something the government doesn't like gets out in our videotape, it is Linh's job on the line. He is not as concerned about the photos we will take, nor the story I will write. It's easy to dismiss those as subjective or biased. What they don't want are Vietnamese people speaking their minds to foreign cameras. Real people voicing real concerns or complaints are more difficult for the government to officially deny.

I'd agreed to the arrangement since it was the only way we'd be allowed in. At one point, suffering from bureaucratic overload, I'd considered—and investigated—the possibility of "sneaking" into the country, with kayaks, and trying to pull of the exploration without official approval. But when I ran the idea by several friends living and working in Vietnam they all said, Sure, you can do that. But it's guaranteed you will be stopped within the first twenty-four hours by some coast guard, navy, or police and be arrested.

Trickier to negotiate than the filming permit was a visa for my teammate Ngan. Until a few weeks before we arrived it was uncertain if they were going to let her into the country, even though she'd visited for work and as a student many times before.

Allowing her to accompany me was a risk, from the government's perspective. Given her language skills—though she'd grown up in New Orleans her family had spoken Vietnamese all her life—I would not be solely dependent on Linh as a translator. If they allowed her to join me, the FPC was ceding a certain amount of control. They took another tactic, attempting to discourage her from coming by asking, as a condition of granting her a visa, for a list of names and addresses of any and all relatives still living in Vietnam. "They've never asked that before," she told me when I relayed the request. "And I've been back into the country twenty times." She took it as a threat and was initially reluctant to give them the list, considering that many of her relatives had been active in South Vietnamese politics and religion and that many had already suffered through postwar "reeducation" camps. I did my best to assure her the government's threat was toothless . . . even though I had no idea if it was or not.

Ultimately Linh got good recommendations from others he'd accompanied. Born and raised in Hanoi, he was just three years old when the American War ended. But sitting in the great room of the crumbling French colonial building, I get the sense he has no clue what we actually want to do, that is kayak the coastline. As we talk, and despite my months of previous communication with him, I sense he sees our adventure as a series of day trips, rather than one long coastal journey. He has already been in contact with local provincial governments and Communist Party representatives along our route, forewarning them that we are coming. He explains that at each stop we will be expected to pay homage to the local party, military, police, etcetera, that have graciously allowed us into its province. Those visits, I already know, will require more endurance than paddling twenty-five miles.

Standing and shaking hands, Linh and I agree to meet in two hours at the Dan Chu Hotel to go over a final itinerary and exchange the first envelope of cash. When he meets me at the hotel's restaurant, the first words out of his mouth are: "I'm afraid I have some bad news."

It is not the last time I would hear that sentence from him.

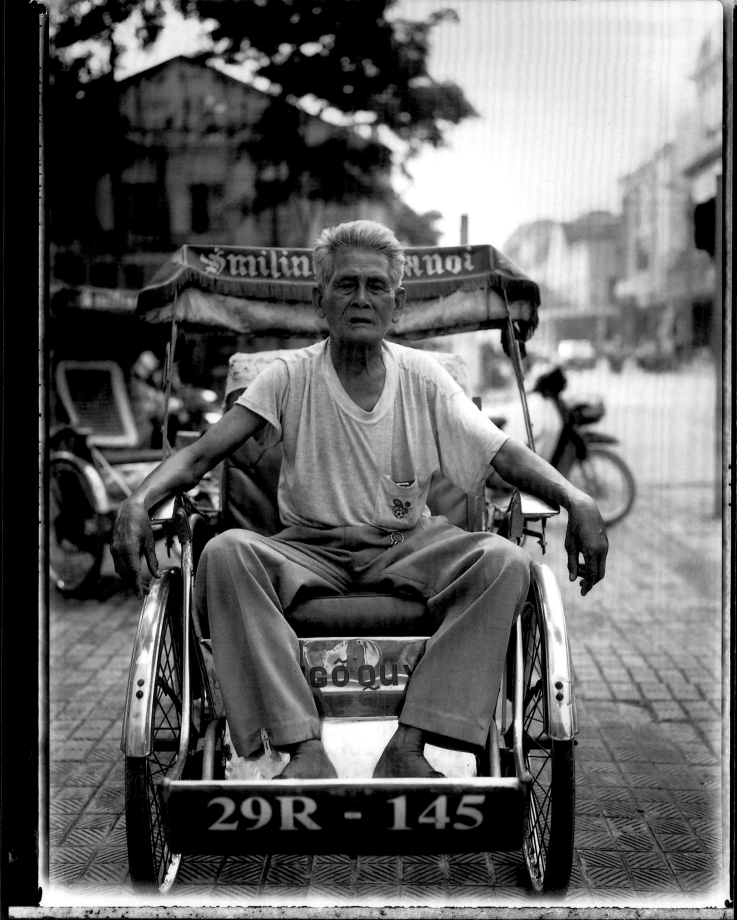

Hanoi

· ·

★H ANOI IS MY FAVORITE big city in Asia for the fact that it hasn't
yet succumbed to the skyscraper competition, which dominates horizons from Singapore to Kuala Lumpur and includes Saigon
(Ho Chi Minh City). I'm partial to Paris and Washington, D.C., too, and
what the three share in common are French planners. In Paris no building can be taller than the Sacre Coeur, in Washington the U.S. Capitol,
in Hanoi there can be nothing taller than the peak of Ho Chi Minh's
cement mausoleum. The result in all three cities is wide, leafy streets and
big, open skies occasionally giving you the feeling that you're not actually
in a city of 4 or 12 million people.

Ho Chi Minh's mausoleum is a stark, dramatic surprise. Its tall,
peaked roof is supported by a phalanx of columns, everything cement
gray. On most days a long line stretches around it, happy to wait more
than three hours to get in. The line is composed mostly of Vietnamese,
primarily from the north, come to pay homage to the man many regard
as the nation's spiritual hero, if not its father. Inside under glass lies Ho
himself. Pale, so harshly lit from above that he appears green and translucent, every couple years his body is sent to Moscow to be reembalmed.
A single file line snakes through the room, kept moving smartly by guards
with big batons. Next door is the simple, two-floor bamboo home on
stilts where he lived, and governed from, for more than twenty-five years.
It is fittingly simple for a proud Communist leader, with one big room for

*Cyclo drivers are among the hardest
workers in Hanoi; this gentleman
camped outside our hotel for hours
waiting to help us.*

Ho Chi Minh's mausoleum is among the most visited tourist sites in Vietnam.

official meetings below, a small office and a bedroom above. He died here in 1969, six years before "his" army was victorious over the south.

I climb to the top of a roof in Hanoi's Old Quarter for a look out over the city, toward its extremities. The wide Red River flows nearby, a rich, muddy brown. I'm six stories off the pavement and surrounded by tall, skinny residential buildings, most with shiny silver solar water tanks squeezed onto small, crowded balconies. All the remaining remnants of French colonial architecture feel warm and welcoming, taking the edge off what at street level often feels intense, jam-packed, and earsplitting. Hanoi will celebrate its millennial birthday in 2010 and there are plans for new bridges, tall buildings, an international athletic complex, and more. The rusting bridge crossing the Red River—designed and constructed by the builders of the Eiffel Tower—is crumbling, accessible only to pedestrians and bicyclists. The French have offered to reconstruct it for the city's anniversary, but the Vietnamese government has proudly said, "No, we can do it ourselves."

Back at street level it is Sunday, hardly a day of rest in this mostly Buddhist nation. I drop into a *bia hoi*—which literally translates as "fresh beer"—one of the ubiquitous bars in Hanoi that serves beer from a keg delivered that morning, which is why they are often crowded early in the day, with local patrons desirous of the freshest pull. On the sidewalk a team of women in blue smocks, conical hats, and face masks squat on their haunches laying red bricks into soggy cement. One of them keeps a cat tied by a purple ribbon to a tree. We are just a few doors away from the small cell where John McCain was imprisoned for seven years. Half a dozen men in their sixties sit in tiny plastic chairs on the sidewalk, slurping *pho* (soup) doled out by a woman their contemporary. When not serving, she loads a bong with tobacco and passes it around.

Government billboards still boast Uncle Ho's image, although he's been dead since 1969.

Military men are ever present across the country.

As daylight fades on the sultry spring afternoon, the beer garden grows more crowded. Motos pull to the door; riders dismount and hand over keys to a pair of valets in matching red T-shirts who scribble an identifying number on the seat in white chalk. A couple, she in a red flannel shirt and blue flannel pants, he in a "Meet the Future" T-shirt and freshly blackened shoes. A father and son lighting cigarettes shaken from the same pack, both wearing the clear plastic sandals that seem to be uniform throughout Vietnam. The smoke from tables of young men and women snakes up the tree in the center of the room that grows through its metal roof, the din in the room growing as the light fades.

Talking with the men at the bar I'm struck by the fact, as I often am in Vietnam, that if the calendar were reversed twenty-five years I could not have safely walked these streets. And the threat would have come from these very men I'm now sitting shoulder to shoulder with, or perhaps their fathers. Right or wrong, the images burnished into my memory when I think of Vietnam are of napalm and bamboo prisons; of bloodied soldiers, their intestines hanging out, lying on a wet jungle floor; of smoke and fire, anger and resentment, the whir of helicopter blades and explosions, the screams of young children and old women running from the fight, crackling radio calls calling in more bombings. One of my desires, one of my reasons for being here, is to replace those media images with a more real set. I am ready to speak with everyone I meet along the route about anything but war.

"Where you from?" asks the man to my right, twirling his half-full glass of beer. He raises his glass to clink with mine. He is a few years older than me.

"Oh, America . . . ," he says, with a big smile. "What a great country. I will go there one day . . . I hope."

I am waiting for a friend, Qiang, who is late. "Sorry! The girl in the real estate office thought I was too handsome, which slowed me down," he offers as an excuse when he rushes through the door. Qiang asks his friends to call him Tiger, for a vague resemblance to the famous golfer.

"I'm trying to buy land—forty-two square meters—and I need some of your luck! So that I can be happy! The real estate girl was helping me with my luck!" Owning your own apartment or house in Vietnam is a recent luxury and though he is young, just thirty, he's climbing the ladder quickly. The place he's hoping for is a narrow, two-story house forty-five minutes out of central Hanoi.

"Historically," he says, pulling up a stool, "the three most important things for a man in Vietnam, in order, were to buy a buffalo—which has now become a moto—build a house, and marry. I've done that in reverse! No moto, you don't go anywhere. Mine was a gift. My father-in-law gave it to us when we were married, so we could go to work. A Honda Dream. So when people ask why I got married, I say it was for the Dream!"

His own father was in the military, for twenty-seven years. When he retired he worked in a steel company for another five years, before quitting work for good. His mother is the family's breadwinner, working for a lamp company, which helped them buy their apartment. Qiang represents a new style of Vietnamese, a hustler with wide knowledge of the world.

"I am lucky already," says Qiang. "My mother had a brother who was a provincial governor and he was very corrupt. He owned many houses and apartments and sold me one for five thousand bucks, payable over twenty years! What luck! Now I am selling it to buy a house." When excited, he shakes his bristle-cut head violently from side to side, just once or twice, as if trying to unloosen something upstairs, or shake something out, like a boxer preparing for round three. With a shake of the head, just like that, he's out on the street buying us egg rolls from a woman cooking over a gas stove on the curb, returning with a half dozen in an oil-stained brown paper sack. I ask how the new government is doing. Unlike any country in the world, other than China, Vietnam is attempting to blend a free market economy with Communist leadership. It is a tricky balancing act and I'm curious what its citizens make of the effort.

"Well, these new guys have only been in for two years," Qiang says of the president and his prime minister. "But I like them. Because it appears they write their own speeches. Not like before where the politicians were just handed papers minutes before a speech by the party and told to read them. These guys seem to have a little more independence.

"And they are far less corrupt than the guys before. Which is one reason you see more and more market growth here." Vietnam's middle class is making modest gains; though the majority of Vietnam's 85 million still live hand-to-mouth.

How corrupt are the new guys? "Well, first, understand that I think small corruption is acceptable. They don't get paid that much anyway. And corruption provides a certain order. Of course I may be a little biased since I have family members in the government.

"What we don't want is to go the way of Russia, where there is far too much corruption in private hands, where it can't be controlled. My attitude is let's keep corruption in the government, where it can be controlled by voting them in, or out."

Washing down the last egg roll with a now warm beer, Qiang is out the door as quickly as he came in. "Have to go visit my grandmother. She's 102, 103 years old. We're not sure exactly since there were no records made when she was born. I'm her favorite grandchild. She's of the generation that chewed betel nut all her life and as a result has black teeth and very red lips. One time I told her it didn't look very good for kissing and she called me a bastard and chased me out of the room. But I am still her favorite!"

The next morning the last of my five-person team arrives. The timing is good since we are scheduled to leave for Ha Long Bay and the South China Sea in two days.

Just after nine o'clock I walk to the unoccupied, dingy, and dimly lit first floor office where the kayaks are stored. I had sent them by ship six months before, and the route to Vietnam had taken more than three months, including a long, unplanned truck ride when they were mistakenly delivered to Ho Chi Minh City rather than Hanoi (like being dropped in Miami when you need them in Boston). Nine hundred dollars later they were in Hanoi. Whenever I have shipped kayaks around the world I cross my fingers they'll arrive. So far, so good, though the boats intended for Gabon ended up in Ivory Coast by mistake, and those I shipped for an Antarctic expedition were held up in a container strike in Peru for several nerve-racking weeks.

A curious throng of Vietnamese peer in the open door as I peel away the cardboard and bubble wrap to have a look at the bright orange, red, and yellow plastic boats. The unwrapping comes with a big sigh of relief. Not just that the boats are here intact, but more because the unveiling means the fun part, the reward, is about to begin. After more than two years of planning, logistical wrangling, team choosing, money raising, government hand-holding, and route making, with-in forty-eight hours we'll actually be afloat. Being on the water at sea level off the coast of Vietnam is my payoff. Not to mention that it will happily take us away from the nonstop horn braying that dominates Hanoi.

I'm accompanied to the kayak storeroom by Lap, the fixer who will accompany us for the duration of the trip. On top of the FPC monitor Linh, I've had to hire a full-time man to coordinate our travel. If Linh and the Central Committee members who will invariably come to greet—and follow us—along the way need a boat, Lap is the man. If we need to circumvent a particular stretch of sea, like Haiphong Harbor, which the government is forbidding us to paddle across due to the heavy big-ship traffic, Lap will find us a truck. Need a hotel along the route, just ask Lap. When I asked Linh why he couldn't perhaps do that job as well, he tsk-tsked. "I will be too busy," he replied.

In a black Puma ball cap and windbreaker, a smile breaching his wide face, Lap is happy to be joining the upcoming adventure, if just to get away from the big city for a while. Yet it's clear as he studies a three-page printout of our planned itinerary that he's never seen it before, even though I've been talking with his boss for more than a year. "You are going to kayak?"

I've been bunkered down at the Dan Chu for a couple weeks, happy for its spacious-if-aged rooms, windows that open wide over the busy street below, and a courtyard where we can spread our gear. We gather as a team for the first time around a table beneath a leafy shade tree. I unroll a thick bundle of maps.

I'd only met filmmaker Peter Getzels once before, at National Geographic headquarters in Washington, D.C., about a month ago. A veteran documentary filmmaker who grew up in Chicago but has lived in the U.K. for the past dozen years, he's a new hire by National Geographic Television. Since this is his first job for them as both producer and videographer, his normally wired personality is clearly even more wired. Bright and fast-talking, an admitted obsessive-compulsive, I have no idea what it's going to be like to travel with him much less work together. (The National Geographic producer/shooter assigned to the job a year ago had bailed out just weeks before, when I couldn't guarantee he'd be home for two annual events he hated to miss, Passover and the New Orleans Jazz Festival.)

Like each of us, Peter's life is spent mostly on the road (he's the father of two girls, his wife also a filmmaker) and he's just completed a Cambodia–U.K.–Portland–Chicago–New Orleans road trip. When he arrived yesterday he was worn out, not in the best of moods. "I travel too much to put up with a dingy hotel room. . . . I need to be focusing on putting my kit together, not putting that bloody kayak together. . . . " were his first comments to me. Hopefully a long, prescription drug induced sleep will help him reset his clock.

Photographer Rob Howard was also a last-minute replacement. For the previous decade I had worked and traveled often with California-based photographer Barry Tessman and he'd been in on the planning of the Vietnam adventure from the beginning. Sadly, six weeks before we were scheduled to fly to Hanoi, he drowned in a mysterious kayak accident on a cold reservoir near his home in Kernville, California. I had flown immediately to the scene of the accident and along with another twenty friends spent days searching for him. All that was found was his racing kayak afloat and upright in the middle of the lake. When I left his house, and his pregnant widow, Joy, that weekend, she pointed out the propped-open book on his bedside table, a collection of Vietnam report-

Merchants sell everything from vegetables to haircuts along Hanoi's busy street curbs.

The easiest way to see Hanoi is by cyclo.

ing that I had sent him, his reading glasses holding his place. It would be a different trip without my good friend.

Like Peter, I had met Rob just once before, in his New York City apartment. Though I knew his work—at that time he'd shot more covers for *Outside* magazine than any other photographer and was working now for the slickest travel magazines and high-end travel companies—we'd had all of an hour together. I loved his portrait work and invited him to join us on the strength of his beautiful, often black-and-white portraits of people. Along the coast we would be meeting thousands of people— fishermen, politicians, beachcombers—and I sensed he would bring back a truly special look at the people who live in the little-seen corners of Vietnam we hoped to visit. He'd backed out of a couple better-paying jobs to come along and had gotten his head nearly shaved in anticipation of several weeks where daily showering was not guaranteed. Toronto-born, he was also just off the road, though his route had been slightly more upscale, swinging him through Whistler, British Columbia, St. Moritz, and New Zealand.

Barry had introduced me to white-water kayaker Polly Green. When considering a team, I was insistent that it be gender-blended; I did not want us to be five big white American men strolling into some of these remote, north Vietnamese villages where the last big white American men they probably saw were wearing camouflage and carrying big guns. I wanted us to present a softer image. Just finishing a winter season of white-water kayaking in Bhutan and New Zealand, Polly also brought with her a revitalizing enthusiasm occasionally missing from the forty-plus-year-olds among us (Peter, Rob, myself), who'd grown a bit jaded from our varying lives of work and travel. That her father had served in Vietnam in the mid-1960s, based in Da Nang, gave her an added curiosity about the country. Coming along had opened a new door for her and her father, giving them a new experience to share.

I also invited twenty-nine-year-old, Durango-based Polly for selfish reasons, which I sketched out in brief before we arrived and more specifically once we were in Hanoi. "Watch Ngan!" I explained to Polly when she asked what her assignment would be.

Though an incredible asset to our quintet, the one area of expertise Ngan lacks is in the kayaking department. Truth is, she'd barely kayaked. And, she wasn't much of a swimmer. We were about to move eight hundred miles down the coastline of her native land. One of Polly's jobs was to help teach Ngan about kayaking and keep an eye on her when we were on the water.

Why invite a non-swimming, non-kayaking woman to join the team?

I barely gave it a second thought. Ngan was so good on all the other fronts—language, knowledge of the culture, history, politics, and environmental issues—that I was interested in, plus her obvious self-determination, I knew we could teach her the skills necessary to stay afloat, if not always upright.

Just twenty-nine years old, Ngan had recently quit her job with the aid agency OXFAM International, would be married a few weeks after we return from Vietnam, and is moving to London soon after.

I found her through a New York City–based newsletter circulated to resettled Vietnamese living in the U.S. When I recognized that I needed a Vietnamese-speaking teammate I advertised for someone who knew the language and the culture and wanted to join a National Geographic sea kayaking expedition.

I received sixty-two responses. Half were from men, which I threw out for the aforementioned gender-blending desire. Of the women, half were Americans living and working in Vietnam, the other were Vietnamese scattered all around the world. I met and interviewed a half dozen, both in the States and during a scouting trip to Hanoi. Ngan stuck out, both for her experience—she'd been to Vietnam more than twenty times, most recently as an aide to then First Lady Hillary Clinton—and desire.

Her story, as I learned from my interviewing, was somewhat typical for the hundreds of thousands of South Vietnamese who fled their homeland during the last days of fighting in 1975. She had fled Saigon with her family on the last day of the war (her father was a helicopter pilot with the South Vietnamese Army). That harrowing escape was followed by a month-long adventure at sea, which eventually delivered them to New Orleans.

She had returned to Vietnam for the first time when she was twenty, accompanying a group of Harvard professors. When she arrived that time she'd been held in a room with one-way mirrors as government officials queried her about her extended family—grandparents, uncles, aunts—still living in Vietnam, many still considered leftists. Many of her family members were involved in the Cao Dai religion, which has 2 to 3 million followers in Vietnam and which the government allows but with tight restrictions. (Her father was its top minister in the U.S.)

"It was classic," she remembers. "It was a dirty white room with a wall of mirrors, which of course they were watching me from behind. There was one dim lightbulb with a microphone in it. I was tempted to pull it down and say 'testing, testing, testing.'

"They wanted to know what I was doing in Vietnam—of course they knew the answers, I'd brought a group of professors from Harvard over for research. They wanted to know who my father was—of course they knew exactly who he was. They eventually pulled out newspaper clippings from a folder, stories published in the U.S. about his ministry.

Jon, writing aboard
a junk afloat on the
Perfume River

Following spread: Family
rowboats move through
the limestone islands of
Ha Long Bay.

Our government monitor, Linh, does his job.
Opposite: Vietnamese-American Ngan Nguyen pulls
her kayak to the sea at China Beach.

Following spread: Polly and Jon navigate through
the port at Cat Ba.

Paddling beneath a bay filled with fishing nets at Lang Co

Opposite: Young clam fishermen on the beach north of Da Nang

Following spreads: Vietnam's youth under 25, who make up a third of the population, infuse the country with energy and optimism.

Women sorting the day's catch for market at Dong Hoi

*Above and opposite: This
family in Ken Ga invited us
in for tea and conversation.*

*Following spread: Looking out
over Ha Long Bay from an
island-top vantage*

They wanted to know what he talked about with his friends. I said, 'I don't know, I haven't lived at home for five years. What do you talk about with your friends?'" On succeeding trips she'd arrived through Laos or Cambodia rather than the States, as a means of appearing less obviously a Viet Khieu—an overseas Vietnamese.

A curious blend of self-described Vietnamese princess and all-American girl she was educated at Tulane and the Fletcher School of Law and Diplomacy in Cambridge, Massachusetts. Charismatic, demanding, suffering from typical refugee confusion ("Am I American? Or Vietnamese?"), her family has deep roots in politics and religion in the Mekong Delta. We would be traveling mostly in the north, which for her had long been considered enemy territory. As comfortable at high tea at London's Four Seasons as on a hard-packed earthen floor in Vietnam drinking from a soiled cup, she self-mockingly describes herself as a "delicate flower." I invited her based on a strong recommendation from a Vietnamese resettlement expert for her knowledge of modern Vietnam.

About her early days in the U.S., where she arrived at age three, she remembers an initial wariness by the Americans she met. "It was hard at first, of course, because we did not feel terribly welcome. Teachers couldn't pronounce my name, so they never called on me. I was nicknamed 'Happy,' because they thought I was always smiling. Initially we lived in a neighborhood where we were the only Vietnamese and whenever a dog in the neighborhood was missing the neighbors knocked on our door, assuming we must have eaten it." She looks away when talking about the racism that greeted her family.

"It wasn't without some humorous moments. When I was a teenager I was teaching English to an older Vietnamese woman just arrived in the country. We were at her house and she had made a dish for lunch and insisted I eat it. I didn't like it, didn't think it tasted good, but to be polite I ate it anyway.

"A week later I took her to the grocery store to do some shopping. When we walked up the aisle selling pet food—you know, canned dog food—she stopped and showed me the variety she'd put into the dish we'd had the week before.

"She thought dog food was . . . well . . . dog. . . . "

That night I organize a dinner to introduce my team to our Vietnamese contingent. The most interesting conversation comes as the table is being cleared, among Ngan, Linh, and Lap, about the current state of affairs in Vietnam. The three are virtually the same age, Ngan and Lap born in 1972, Linh in 1973.

Despite that similarity, the differences in their young lives are stark. She was born in the Mekong Delta; they were both born in Hanoi—all just a few years before the end of the American War. She fled the country and grew up in the U.S. Lap's family owned a leather factory and he remembers hiding from bombs in a shelter under his family house in Hanoi, then being sent to live with uncles in the countryside. Linh's parents were Hanoi schoolteachers, active in the party. "They worked for the ministry of education," he explains, prompting Ngan to whisper behind her hand: "Which means propaganda." She has traveled extensively around the world; they have not yet left Vietnam.

They all agree the necessity for Vietnam today is less disparity between rich and poor and less bureaucracy. The main point of contention is Ngan's belief that what might most help the country is more political choice and a variety of freedoms (like speech, religion, press). Lap and Linh are convinced it is too early to give people in the relatively young country too much choice, or too much freedom.

They also believe today there's little tension between people born in the south and north. Unlike many of her fellow Viet Khieu, Ngan agrees. "In the U.S., most of the 1 million Viet Khieu living there who can vote, vote Republican. Because they want a government that takes a tough approach to Vietnam. Somehow they still want to punish the government. Yet, turn around, and the same Republicans run many of the businesses trying to establish trade with Vietnam. It is very confusing.

"The bottom line is that here we are all Vietnamese, more similar in many ways than different," she says, "no matter which side of the man-made dividing line you were born on."

Lap and Linh are convinced that any problem/threat/concern from the south does not lie with what they call "good" Viet Khieu—tipping their hats to Ngan—but with a "bad" strain, the ones who organize protests in the U.S. against the current government and send "agitators" to Vietnam to spread "trouble." I ask if they can cite an example of such agitation; the only thing they come up with is a recent lone pilot dropping anti-government leaflets over suburban Hanoi.

Polly and I spent the bulk of the next afternoon on our knees on the hotel's brick courtyard, smack between a massage parlor and a classroom teaching "tourist hospitality," assembling our fourth kayak, a nineteen-foot-three-inch Feathercraft K2. A tandem folding kayak with an aluminum frame and yellow hypalon skin, I'd lugged it with me from the States. Wide and sturdy, it would make a great camera boat for Peter and Rob, as well as a safe learning platform for Ngan, with Polly in the stern, guiding and teaching her.

"First time assemblage of double should take 2 hours," promised the instruction manual. Five and a half hours later, much frustrated and including a break for lunch, we successfully stretched the skin over the frame the way its manufacturers had intended. Twice we'd had to pull the frame out of the skin and start over, since the assemblage looked lumpy rather than taut. Part of our problem is that the instruction manual seemed to have been written by either profound experts or brothers from another planet.

"Do we feel like idiots, or what," Polly asks, popping her bushy head out from inside the big cockpit, having finally wrestled the last chine into place and figuring out exactly what the instructions had meant by "make a Velcro sandwich."

The most fun of the afternoon is watching the gathered crowd of Vietnamese men watching us. Cooks from a nearby restaurant in white uniforms, old guys with wispy chin beards, young guys in mismatched suits (green jacket, plaid pants), all commenting on our failing efforts, pointing and laughing at our frustrations.

At one point we have the stern of the aluminum frame mistakenly inserted into the bow of the hypalon skin, at which point the whole folding boat collapses. With that, the crowd can't stand it anymore and dives in to help, pushing us out of the way, elbows pushing, palms hammering, all talking excitedly.

Hands on hips I stand back and watch them now, happy for the break and thrilled that they might figure out what we have obviously been missing.

Within ten minutes they seem to have "forced" the thing together and jump up with great enthusiasm. Clapping each other on the back, still laughing over their accomplishment, they quickly filter out of the courtyard, headed back to work or on their way home. But as soon as Polly and I bend down to admire their handiwork, the aluminum skeleton pops apart.

Later in the afternoon, the folding kayak successfully unfolded, the phone rings in my room. It's Linh. "I have not good news for you," which I already know is his way of saying I have bad news. Though our itinerary had been approved by a variety of government bureaucrats weeks ago, my guess is he's calling to tell me that one or another provincial chieftain or party hack is now saying no to something on our route. Without further detail, he says he'll be right over.

Fifteen minutes later Linh is in the Dan Chu's restaurant, a hot tea already in front of him, waiting for me.

"So, as I said, I have some not so good news." I was absolutely correct. Apparently the party chiefs just north of Da Nang—we had asked approval from ten different provinces along our route—had "misunderstood" Linh's initial asking.

"Remember you asked to leave the lagoon at Thuan and go out onto the sea before returning to the beach at Lang Co? Well, that part of the sea is now off limits to you. Instead, they want you to stay inside the Thuan Lagoon all the way south and maybe—maybe—exit onto the sea at the bottom of the lagoon." The difference is that we would be paddling on a protected area, surrounded by small villages, rather than on the open ocean and sleeping on beaches.

"They apparently did not hear correctly what I said to them the first time," Linh explains. "They think it is very dangerous on the sea and they don't want you to go out there."

This kind of wrangling has been going on for months and now we are on the eve of departure.

"But Linh. These are *sea* kayaks. They are built to be used on the *sea*." No one here seems to trust me when I tell them we'll be fine paddling on the ocean.

"It's difficult, Mr. Jon. Remember most of these people we are asking have no idea what is a sea kayak.

"And actually, I don't think they are worried about you even though they say they are. I think they are worried about their own boats, the ones we'll need to hire in order to follow you."

I've learned in my brief give-and-takes with Linh that I must push, if just a bit, for permission. If not, our sea kayak adventure risks turning into a road trip.

"If you think they are confused, let's ask again."

"If you insist, I will fax them again," he says, stubbing out his cigarette. "I will try and convince them."

I don't believe him. He has already explained that once we leave Hanoi, his power base, we will largely be in the hands of the provincial chiefs. I doubt he'll have much sway over them, in person or by fax. But the system dictates that he must ask, and that they must grant—or deny—permission.

When Linh leaves the coffee shop I move to a table where Peter is having an early dinner. He'd filmed the entire conversation, with Linh's approval.

"I'm beyond disappointment at this stage," I offer. "Now, I just want to get out there, start traveling and push him whenever, wherever we can. I'm afraid if we stay much longer in Hanoi 'negotiating' over what we can and cannot do, where we can and cannot go, soon we'll be down to simply just moving into the Metropole for a month and waiting out the monsoons. . . ."

Ha Long Bay

· ·

★T HE FOUR-HOUR DRIVE from Hanoi to Ha Long Bay winds past a
hundred miles of rice fields separated occasionally by palm
tree forests. Out the truck window I can see the conical hats of women
workers bobbing up and down, hoeing and picking, taking in the second
crop of the calendar year. Rice has been cultivated here for the past nine
thousand years; today Vietnam produces 5 percent of all of the world's
rice (second to China) and is the world's second largest exporter (after
Thailand). Interspersed are fields of corn, sweet potatoes, and sugarcane.
Irrigation is not an issue, though it is a coming fight. Two thousand rivers
crisscross Vietnam and water rights laws are very old and very controversial. Increasingly farmers are leaving rice fields for big cities, leaving for
jobs that pay a hundred dollars a month, which is more than they were
making in the fields.

Beginning just half an hour outside of Hanoi, the fields are also
broken up by sprawling factories, reminiscent of the giant car company
plants that once dominated so many Midwestern U.S. landscapes. But the
products here are not cars but beer, cigarettes, shoes, leather jackets. The
factories are surrounded by mini-villages of three- and four-story brick
houses built for workers, though nearly all are abandoned, on the verge
of collapse. "They could never get people to move out here," says Lap,
who's driving the van. "They'd rather commute an hour each way by
bus and live in Hanoi than out here surrounded by rice fields. What the

*Children make their way to school in
one of Ha Long Bay's floating villages.*

39

factory owners didn't understand is that in like most countries what Vietnamese want is out of the fields and into the cities."

The biggest economies in Vietnam today are, in order, clothes and leather; seafood; natural resources, including coal and gold; rice and tourism. "We export 2 billion dollars of clothes yet 90 percent of the 85 million Vietnamese wear clothes made in China. Something is wrong with that, don't you think?" says Lap.

All along the roadside, scantily clad young girls sit daintily in plastic chairs next to tables heavy with pineapples, coconuts, and bananas. Hmmmm. Using sex to sell. What a novelty! Though the face masks the girls wear against the car and truck exhaust are a bit of a turnoff.

Ha Long City is Vietnam's bizarre equivalent to a giant marine park. Its three-hundred-foot-long main dock is lined with half-day and full-day tourist boats and packed with red-faced day-trippers in baggy shorts from every country on the planet, including, these days, lots of middle-class Chinese.

We will be out on the thousand-square-mile Ha Long Bay for the next ten days. Since there are no beaches to camp on, and very few towns, I've hired a support boat to follow us so that we'll have some place to sleep. Last week I came out and scouted, riding on a pretty, simple junk with classic red sails. It was rudimentary, but perfect for our needs. The kayaks could easily be lashed down to its roof and dropped into the water at the start of each day. A simple kitchen meant we wouldn't go hungry.

But when we arrive, the boat awaiting us is quite different. Apparently the government, that is, the local political party, has decided we—the team from the U.S., from National Geographic—need transportation somewhat more elegant. Waiting for us at the end of the dock is a long line of party officials, leading to the gangway of the fanciest boat on Ha Long Bay. Just four months old, it is all teak and mahogany, with wooden deck chairs, shiny new bathrooms, and white linen on the dining room table. They have failed us upward, as I've seen often in my travels, by thinking that Americans will be disappointed by anything but over-the-top. I protest, quietly but forcefully to Linh, to no avail. I ask for them to go find the simple junk I'd seen the week before. He doesn't even bother to confer. "It's all arranged, too late to change," he says.

We are half an hour behind schedule and Linh is in a small panic because the party committee people have been buzzing his cell phone, wondering where we are. When we walk down the crowded dock, carrying kayaks, it's like a carnival, with flags whipping in a hot wind, music coming off each of the dozens of boats tied to the dock. The pair of brothers who own the boat greet us, as well as several party officials including Mr. Ha, the local party chief. He's dressed up for the occasion, in paisley shirt and striped tie. I joke that I hope he's not disappointed that I didn't have time to change into my tie. I've just learned from Linh—as we walked down the dock—that Mr. Ha will also be accompanying us on the boat through Ha Long Bay, so I figure I better try to impress him in my own meager way.

We all step onto the boat and a silver tray is produced heavily laden with tall glasses and cans of cold Tiger beer. They present each of us with a tourist map and then the toasts begin.

Mr. Ha stands up. He is tall, wearing pilot-shaped bifocals and a blue shirt covered with brown flowers. "We welcome you with all our hospitality and warmth to this great and beautiful place and invite you to visit everywhere with our enthusiastic support, except of course for those places that are prohibited for you to visit." The last will be a recurring theme wherever we go, basically saying we welcome you to our country with open arms but please, Mr. Jon, know that of course you can't go here, can't go there, etcetera, etcetera, etcetera.

Toasts are followed by a sumptuous lunch for fifteen, with all of us—Rob, Peter, Ngan, Polly, and myself—sharing bewildered looks, wondering what kind of spectacle we've stumbled into. No one is more concerned than me by the forced opulence; my goal throughout the trip is to be as inconspicuous as possible, to try as best we can—even though we are admittedly white people traveling in brightly colored kayaks—to meld into the scene. With this boat as our escort, *we* will unfortunately be the story wherever we go. As we finally push away from the dock, I let out a big sigh of relief mixed with some small trepidation, thanks to our monitors (whose numbers appear to be growing), the imposed restrictions, the evermore attempts at control. But I'm happy, too. Finally, we are afloat.

Daybreak, Tu Long Bai, a hundred miles south of the Chinese border. During the night a dense fog set in over the haystack-shaped limestone islands that line the northern coast. On the junk's roof, just beyond its rolled saffron sails where I slept beneath the stars, four shiny kayaks sweat under a morning dew.

A silvery morning dawns as the fog slowly lifts, unveiling layers of the tree-covered stone islands. The sky's clearing is accompanied by the sounds of songbirds, howler monkeys, and the incessant putt-putt of the two-stroke engines that are the lifeblood of these fishing people. We are camped next to a small floating village and morning sounds—Mom's

cooing to an infant, Dad's striking of a hammer, and dogs barking—all echo off the tall cliff walls that surround.

We slip the kayaks onto the glassy, green sea. After the five oceans, the South China Sea is the world's largest body of water. Its importance—economically and strategically—is such that its bordering nations (China, the Philippines, Taiwan, and Vietnam) battle non-stop over who owns it. Its waterways are also among the most pirated in the world. Thankfully for us, pirates are usually after big ships filled with goods and electronics. I can't imagine them wasting too much time with us, just to steal a camera or two. The thirty-five hundred limestone

The best way to maneuver among the houses, school, and shops of a floating village is by rowboat; children who grow up here often learn to swim before they can walk.

islands of Ha Long Bay are probably the best-known geographic image the world has of Vietnam. All around are traces of the giant Descending Dragon after whom these bays are named. It is said to be his enraged thrashings that carved the canyons and hollows in the mountain landscape and allowed the surrounding seas to thunderously rise and flood them. Each fantastically balanced sandstone boulder, each submarine cave and limestone grotto shows the scale print of his writhing. Under the influence of the Cham people, the innovative culture that ruled Vietnam for 1,300 years from the second to fifteenth centuries, the dragon was the country's most influential sysmbol; even its most powerful deity was a dragon figure. Today statues of dragons are still found everywhere along the coast.

As we ready for our first paddle Linh says to me, "Don't go too far away... so that I can properly manage you." I get into my boat and take three strong strokes. Over my waterproof radio, though I am only twenty feet from the support boat, comes Linh's worried voice: "Jon! Jon! Where are you?" It's obvious that he'll take some breaking in.

As I paddle the calm sea this early morning I ponder a question that's been stuck in my head since landing in Hanoi several weeks before: Why are we here? It's a good question and probably not so dissimilar to the very query posed by those quivers of young American soldiers who arrived here thirty-five years ago, many of them against their better judgment.

Then, Vietnam was off limits to visitors other than those in uniform. Today it's high on the list of tourists from around the globe, adventurous and otherwise. They are everywhere now—Europeans, North Americans, Australians, and plenty of Chinese—though traveling in packs, on routes approved by the government in Hanoi. From day trips on Ha Long Bay, to bus tours of Hanoi, visiting the sites of famous battles like Khe Sanh and Hamburger Hill. The Communist government has grudgingly come to accept these strangers, if only for the 2 billion dollars the 4 million visitors carry into the country with them each year.

On this first day, during twenty-five miles of paddling, a sea level panoramic unfolds. We kayak just next to young children clamming in the shallows, a husband and wife net fishing in the middle of a wide bay, men standing balanced in small bamboo boats chipping mussels from the tide-exposed rocks. They use the sea like a piece of farmland, cultivating every corner. But it's not very well taken care of—signs of man litter the green sea. Everywhere floating in the calm are plastic bags, playing cards, rubber thongs, bottles, and more.

At midday under a hot sun I paddle alongside Ngan, who paddles with seeming ease across the glassy surface, despite that this is her first day kayaking on the ocean.

Including Ngan on the team was an imperative for me. With her along we could talk to the people we meet—and we would encounter dozens, hundreds each day—without having to rely on Linh. The last time she was on the water in Vietnam was the day in 1975 when they were helicoptered from Saigon to waiting ships, about a thousand miles south of where we are paddling.

"Basically I became a political refugee at the age of three," she says. "What I remember most about that time was that I had the measles. It was April 30, 1975, and my father—who was a helicopter pilot with the South Vietnamese Army—was allowed to bring his family out to one of the U.S. aircraft carriers sitting on the South China Sea off Saigon.

"For several weeks it was clear the government was going to fall and my father had been planning our escape for a while. But he could only take care of his immediate family, the five of us—my mother, my older sister, me, my younger brother—no other relatives. We only learned of this the day before, on April 29, and I was feverish with the measles.

"Everyone remembers those images? Of helicopters picking people off the roof of the embassy in Saigon, people fighting and crowding to get onto them, then flying out to the waiting carriers, landing, emptying, and the helicopters being pushed overboard to make room for the next one to land? We were part of that scene.

"From that first boat we were moved to a second, a larger boat, and as we transferred by rope ladder, my father carrying my one-year-old brother strapped to his back, the ladder broke, separating them from us.

I remember my father dangling on the rope until others pulled him onboard, my mother looking on in complete panic, thinking she was about to lose half her family.

"For three days we just sat there, the boat didn't move. Finally we headed for the Philippines, which took about twelve days. Everyone on the boat was rationed one bowl of rice a day. Because I was sick people were giving us extra food. Ultimately, once we were in the United States, I would grow up with some of the people we met on that boat, some of them became lifelong friends."

Linh has quickly become a big part of our adventure, just another hurdle to be dealt with on a daily basis, like an incoming wind or rainstorm. His standard uniform in the field is a green army pith helmet, mirrored sunglasses, and a pair of cell phones in carrying cases strapped to his belt. His favorite pastime turns out to be karaoke, his favorite singer Elvis Presley. In fact he likes to think he resembles Elvis and while he is quite short and a little squat, something like a pudgy schoolboy, I can occasionally make out a vague, Vietnam-style similarity. Probably it's the jet-black hair.

He also considers himself quite the lady-killer (though he has a wife and young child at home). His two favorites songs at the karaoke bars, the ones he says truly melt the girls, are "Love Me Tender" and, that traditional heartbreaker, "Edelweiss."

(His approach is admittedly more couth than Lap, who early on in our travels explains what he calls the "Five Cs" that attract a woman to a man: Cash, Car, Credit Cards, Condo, Cock.)

I'm also getting used to the unique rhythm of his English, including the occasional malapropism.

"Okay, take your time please."

"Sleep well. Okay. Take your time."

"See you tomorrow. Okay. Take your time."

"Have a good paddle. Okay. Take your time."

"Okay. See you again in Vietnam. Soon. Take your time."

Limestone rocks jut out of the sea ahead, like turning directionals. Our four kayaks—three single Perception Corona's and one big folding double Feathercraft—are spread out over a quarter mile. To our left, tucked into a protected nook, we can make out some kind of aquaculture. Ropes and buoys stretch in long straight lines and faded turquoise cement buildings dot the shoreline. Communicating by hand signal, we cut toward shore.

As soon as we turn, the radio stuck under the bungee on the front of my boat crackles. "Oh, Mr. Jon. Can you hear me?" It's Linh, watching us from a distance aboard the support boat. He'd finally admitted to me this morning, after my asking him day after day what his "job" was out here tailing us, that it was to "make sure you meet only people who 'tell the truth.'"

Stunned by his admission, and party-indoctrinated naivete, I asked how he recognized a truth-teller from a fiction-weaver, a fabricator, and a liar.

"Trust me, Mr. Jon. I know. And I will make sure you know too!"

Picking up the radio, I respond. "Yes, what is it Linh?"

"Where are you going right now?"

"We're just going in to check out this fish farm."

"That is not a fish farm, that's what I want to tell you."

"Okay. What is it then?"

"It is a pearl farm, and you should not—YOU CANNOT—go in there. The Communist Party and the Chinese own it and it is prohibited for you to enter. Just stay where you are." We are already deep inside the boundaries, kayaks floating over taut ropes.

Innocently we had entered our first prohibited area.

"I am sure the security people will not be happy to see you," Linh continues.

Sure enough, even as he speaks out roars a big metal motorboat carrying a pair of bare-chested and muscled twenty-year-olds. From our sea-level perspective it is impossible to see inside their deep-hulled bow but, by the way Linh had used the word "security," I am sure some kind of weaponry lay at their feet.

Ngan tries to explain to them that we are just curious, asking what they are growing, where they are from. They refuse to answer, motioning with their hands: *GO AWAY.* Rob tries to warm them up by paddling over and extending a hand. No response, just cold stares.

In floating homes, labor typically divides along gender lines: The men fish, while the women tend to the home and sell the fish.

Cued by their menacing look, we retreat. On the perimeter of the small bay we paddle past a small black flag attached to a buoy.

"It's probably mined," I shout to Ngan.

"That's no joke," she replies, steering clear of the buoy. "In Cambodia they do that all the time, put mines around government-owned or off-limit properties."

For the rest of the day I'm imagining the tip of my kayak tripping a waterborne mine, sending bright red and yellow plastic shrapnel high into the sky.

The first time I saw Ha Long Bay was in the black of night, a year before. I had come to scout and had hired a small boat out of Haiphong Harbor. Along the way I remember paying "tolls" at various points during the night, which involved smaller boats racing alongside, throwing lines onto our boat, and us tossing down coins. The only light came from the powerful halogens aboard squid boats shining brightly into the dark sea to attract their catch. I wouldn't see the tall, limestone islands streaked with pale yellow stripes, birds soaring above their greenery, until morning. Arriving that way—waking up surrounded by the calm, very green sea, limestone island folding into limestone island, a pale blue sky ribboned by corduroy cirrus clouds, rock walls worn down by centuries of winds and tides creating caves and sculptured cornices—planted a powerful memory. The sound of that morning stayed with me too, particularly the ever present *tik-tik-tik-tik-tik-tik* of the rudimentary two-stroke engines that power each of the hundreds of wooden fishing boats.

Fishing is *the* economy out here and we find small boats anchored or trolling around every corner. A solo man waits in the shallows, a blue plastic tarp stretched over a pair of low, U-shaped bamboo poles giving him some shade, surrounded in his boat by a variety of netting tools. Two men, father and son, the older man in a once white dress shirt, his son sporting a dark sports jacket, row slowly, dragging several fishing lines, a cook fire leaping from the bottom of their boat, readying morning tea. Another lone man in a conical hat hand lines in front of the rocks as the tide rolls in, twirling a weighted line in the air above his head, like a cowboy readying to lasso a calf, sending it straight toward the limestone wall before it plunks into the glassy sea, over and over and over. A mom and pop work a small boat, each grasping an oar in weathered hands— he from the back, she on the starboard side–to give the boat small momentum. A blue tarp is neatly rolled and stored to one side, protection for when the daily rains come; a tired orange plastic bucket sits on the floor, for bailing; threadbare laundry hangs on the back of the boat, drying. He slowly pulls in a net by hand; she scoops with a hand net. All around them small glassine fish jump, hundreds at a time. I ask what they call the small jumping fish. He looks quizzically, then answers, "We call them . . . jumping fish!"

About twenty-six hundred people live in communities of floating houses scattered around Ha Long Bay. Turning a corner and coming up on one of them for the first time is stunning. What an ingenious idea! Rent is free. Fishing is right out the front door. And every house has its own fish farm, which doubles as a front porch.

Cua Van, for example, is home to two hundred families, more than seven hundred people in all. Eighteen miles from Ha Long City, it covers nearly fifty acres of sea and has been around in some form or another for a thousand years.

The plywood and two-by-four houses, floated on empty plastic barrels and giant blocks of Styrofoam, come with a variety of amenities, ranging from hammocks and satellite dishes, to dogs and television sets. Kids are often born on boats and learn to swim before they can read. The more prosperous have a small squid boat tied to the dock. Virtually all keep a pen of fish beneath the floorboards of the front porch, which they grow to sell twice a year at market in Ha Long City. Fresh water is a big necessity and is delivered from the mainland every couple weeks by a big cement boat. Boatbuilding is both art and business. The typical twelve-foot-long bamboo boat is built of aged wood, its hull coated with asphalt. It generally lasts three to five years, but is the lifeblood of these communities.

Tourism is booming in Ha Long Bay, too booming in fact. In 2001 there were a hundred boats working out of Ha Long City, in 2007 there are more than five hundred. Just how big is tourism getting? Chinese are starting to bring cruise boats, with several hundred passengers each.

Pet dogs may seem out of place in the floating villages; they are, however, quite common.

While tourism is a growing economy and many are trying to cash in, everyone fishes, using techniques passed down through the centuries.

Big wooden sticks (*bo go*) are banged together just above the water to attract fish, mostly mullet. Hand lines are wrapped around wooden spools. Handmade wooden lures are used for squid. Using bamboo fish traps (*lo*) they catch shellfish and mollusks; on tidal flats and reefs and in the mangroves they use shovels to dig up beach worms; when the tide drops—more than six feet in some places—they take out tiny chisels and chip oysters, mussels, and clams off the rock walls. With two-and three-pronged metal spears they go after *ca song* (grouper) and *ca hong* (red snapper). They cast with dragnets of all shapes and sizes—triangles, rectangles, squares, round. Unraveling and repairing nets is a full-time job, using a long metal hook (*nan can*). Every day these fishermen pray to water nymphs with the Disneyesque names of Mr. Song and Mr. Be, burning joss sticks in their honor, especially during family weddings, funerals, or illness.

The tourist boom has created a cottage industry in the small wooden boats (*mung ban hang*) that—like floating 7–11s—sell anything and everything anyone might need. One hazy morning, Polly and I stop and visit with a woman in her forties slowly oaring her twelve-foot-long floating store in a quiet bay, waiting for a tourist boat to pass. Black hair pulled into a tight bun, she wears matching red-and-yellow-flowered top and pants and a black sweater. The boat's green paint is long faded, but its inventory is immaculately ordered.

She must squat low on her haunches to move beneath the black tarp that protects her shop from the elements, resembling a super-lithe insect as she maneuvers around the tight space whisking it clean. In neat lines are stacked bags of potato chips and Oreos, chewing gum and cooking oil, instant soups, tamarind, cabbage, tomatoes, limes, broccoli, carrots, ginger, leeks, sweet potatoes, cantaloupes. Bottled water is a big item with tourists; for locals she pours water straight from a plastic jug. Cigarettes are her biggest seller. On the back of the boat she cuts fresh vegetables and boils water for soup and tea. She'll sell some to the tourists—and stocks painted oyster shells and strands of freshwater pearls for them—but her real business comes from the crews working the dozens of tourist junks she'll see in a day.

When we turn a corner and paddle into Vong Vieng, a heavy mist hangs over the village of nearly eight hundred people, living in 128 floating homes. Though fishermen have used this hideaway behind the tall rocks for a century, this is a newer town, the houses shinier, constructed within the past ten years. They are permanent, 365-days-a-year residences but if necessary—say a typhoon is on its way—anchors can be lifted and the houses towed closer to the rocks for more protection.

The first man we meet is Nguyen Van Nuoi, a ninety-year-old father of ten. Long-faced, with earlobes stretching nearly to his chin, he tell us he's outlived two wives and credits his good health to a seafood diet, herbal medicines, and never touching his lips to cigarettes or alcohol. He's lived in these bays for more than sixty years and remembers working as a messenger for the communists when the French were fighting here in the 1940s. During the sixties he says the Americans bombed here with regularity, attempting to break up the delivery of food and weapons along the Ho Chi Minh Sea Trail, forcing locals to hide their boats in caves during the day and fish only at night. "The Viet Cong and American Navy warships played cat-and-mouse in and out of these islands," he remembers. As we talk, the village's fishing boss comes by, spiral notebook in hand, inquiring how Van's fifty-seven-year-old son fared the night before. The old man lifts up a board in his porch, reaches down and pulls out a crab the size of his hand. "It was a good night," he says.

We ask what's new in town and he points to a slightly bigger floating compound two "doors" down. "The school," he says, waving goodbye.

Le Thi To Nga is the state-supported teacher overseeing the year-old, eighty-student, floating schoolhouse. Its three teachers are sent from the mainland, salaries paid by the government in Hanoi. Students are from six years old to fifteen; after that very few go on to more schooling, most of the young men head off to sea.

Classrooms are filled with small, blue plastic chairs. On the walls are tall blackboards, Communist Party posters featuring a young girl in uniform holding a big bouquet of yellow flowers, and a gold-framed photo of Ho Chi Minh. Kids arrive from around the bay each morning by 7 A.M., either rowed by parents or grandparents or paddling their own rafts made from chunks of thick, white Styrofoam or pieces of plank tied together by wire. At 7:01 the calm bay that surrounds the classroom is filled with the sound of the morning song, a daily ritual tribute to Uncle Ho.

An arm draped around the shoulder of her prize student, Nga explains why she decided to come here to teach, despite the more than occasional boredom of being young and living in a place where if you step off the porch you drop into a two-thousand-foot-deep sea. Her home is a simple room behind one of the classrooms; her friends are mostly the young wives of fishermen left behind for days and nights while the squid boats are at sea.

"Though I was born inland I now feel part of the sea," says Nga. "Whenever I go home I am ready to come back within a few days." The paucity of young people her age—especially young men—is a deterrent to staying for long. "Most of the young guys work on fishing boats and go to sea for two and three months." But her toughest assignment is just keeping kids coming to school. "The parents sometimes get lazy, don't want to row them here and pick them up each day, even though for most it is only a ten-minute exercise."

Next door is another recent addition to the village, a karaoke bar, lit up at night with Christmas lights. She says everyone except the old folks and "good girls" go nightly to the bar. "It's the only relief from boredom we have," she admits. Every night the bay is put to sleep by the sound of karaoke singing and a thumping disco beat.

She introduces us to her best friend, Luyen. Mother of one, widowed at thirty-one, from her floating house she runs a small aquaculture business (fish farm) with the help of two young cousins and her brother. "Our business is growing fast," she says, "thanks to you guys—tourists!" Her specialty is big fish, which can grow to two hundred pounds and which she can sell for $350 in Hanoi. Her monthly profit after paying off interest on a loan arranged by the local party is a hundred dollars, which she splits with her parents on the mainland.

Rough wooden planks tied securely in neat squares separate the twenty or so holding ponds where her fish grow. She uses no chemicals, no steroids, and no fertilizers, which is contrary to the trend of her neighbors and nearby bays, where big aquaculture companies are moving in fast all along the coast, forcing out small family operations and pumping farmed fish—and thus the surrounding seas—full of unnatural substances.

A pretty woman with flat features, she wears a green-and-white sweater over gray sweatpants. A widow for six years—her husband was killed in a motorcycle accident on the mainland—she keeps insisting she is not pretty and that she would love to make an American baby. She also comments several times on how soft and "full" we Americans are, compared to Vietnamese like herself who are thin, sun-hardened.

Squatting, balanced on just a thin plank inches above the bay, she pulls a fresh fish out of a tank and insists we stay for breakfast. Her younger brother hustles about for some vegetables and we are welcomed into their one-room house for some prebreakfast tea and rice wine. "Drink," she says of the wine, "it will help with your digestion. Plus, it is made by our mother, so it has no chemicals either." It does taste different than others we've been offered, which tended to taste like lighter fluid.

Outside there are potted plants on the porch; inside the walls are covered with pictures of young women cut from magazines. A small turquoise plastic cup is nailed to the wall, holding toothpicks. Cracks between the floorboards serve equally well as ashtray and a depository for cups of tea grown cold. The radio plays scratchy music, interrupted by the occasional news report.

Once it's established we are Americans, they want to know what we think of our president and his seeming penchant for war.

"What is it with America and war?" she asks, ironic coming from the mouth of a north Vietnamese. "Wouldn't it be good if your country would just stay at home, stay at peace for awhile? Don't you learn from the past?"

Former President Bill Clinton and his family had recently visited Vietnam and they had listened to his speeches on the radio. "He was a good President," says one cousin, his tone suggesting he doesn't have the same confidence in his successor.

"But still, he was no Uncle Ho!"

Small, silvery fish jump by the hundreds over my bow as we pull into a channel dividing the island village of Cong Dau Ty. People have lived on these distant islands, far to the east in Ha Long Bay, for centuries. This one was most recently repopulated in 1960 when the government resettled it to get people off an already crowded mainland. The town's name—which translates as Victory—came from locals having successfully participated in the wars that beat back the Japanese, the French, the Americans, and, finally, the Chinese. The name of the village reminds me of a line in *Apocalypse Now,* when Captain Willard remarks there are only two ways for North Vietnamese to go home: "With death . . . or victory."

Pulling my boat onto the muddy tidal flats, I am greeted by a man in a blue zip-up pullover, green pants cuffed high to avoid the muck, and blue plastic sandals. Thin, with a thick shock of black hair and prominent, tanned cheekbones, he introduces himself as Toan, thirty years old, from Hanja, a small village on the mainland.

A kind of traveling alternative-medicine man he owns no boat and no home, drifting from town to town, Johnny Appleseed–like, carrying

Children attend government-financed schools in the floating villages; most quit before they are sixteen years old.

only a big burlap bag packed with various woods, roots, leaves, and seeds he uses to cure everything from kidney stones to malaria, strokes to ailing livers. In Victory he is living in a borrowed stucco house on the opposite side of the river; he invites us to paddle him across to see his herb garden and watch him prepare some medicines. We have successfully ditched our monitor for the day and happily accept. This is a particularly old and off-the-beaten-path place; in the mud all around where we walk are centuries-old pottery chards from a time when Vietnam competed with China to produce some of the finest pottery in the world. Ngan and I pick up small pieces to carry back to the States for carbon dating.

His borrowed house is surrounded by neat gardens, fertilized by ash. Palm trees rise on the hill behind. A constant and smoky fire helps keep the bugs away. On the porch hang a worn hammock and his clothes—three pairs of pants and three shirts. A pair of doorways enters the white stucco building, though there are no doors. Inside is simply a bed, mosquito netting draped over it.

His medicines are neatly stored around the room. On a rack above his bed small plastic shopping bags are filled with various herbs and wood shavings. On the floor a newspaper is covered by a neat pile of what looks like finely cut tea. In the open rafters are stuck big, gnarled tree roots and limbs.

He has a mission, to ready nine daily portions of a concoction for a client suffering from bad kidneys.

On the rough cement floor he lays out nine perfectly square pieces of newsprint and begins. From one plastic bag then another he scoops a seemingly random pinch of crushed leaves, ground roots, and herbs into neat piles on each paper. Reaching deftly beneath his straw mattress, he pulls out a straight-bladed machete, and then wrestles a twisted tree root down from the rafters. Resting one end of the root on the floor, he methodically whittles it down to nothing, talking all the while, barely watching what he's doing, expertly avoiding shaving flesh off his leg while he hacks.

While he cuts he fills in his life story. He'd been in the army until he was twenty-three, fighting against the Chinese near the border at Mong Cai, a conflict that lasted into the 1990s. Like so many people we had already met in the north, he had tried several times, by boat, to escape the poverty and desperate times that still rack postwar Vietnam. He was caught and returned each time. In retrospect he is glad he wasn't successful. "There are so many poor people here who can't afford the help of a traditional doctor, it is good that I am here. I am better and more affordable."

Curatives prepared, we paddle back across the channel and follow him up a crushed-dirt path past neat cement, nearly square houses and curious stares. These villagers have never talked with, nor touched the hand of an American. During the war, Ha Long Bay was heavily bombed, in part because it was home to the Ho Chi Minh Sea Trail, over which weapons, ammunition, and food were carried by boat to overland fighting units.

We are welcomed into the home of Cua, sixty-three, and his wife, Loi, sixty-two. He is dark and wiry and full of spunk (or is it rice wine?). She is pretty, wearing a black velvet scarf, a yellow sweater pulled over a pink T-shirt and brown flowered pants. Both are barefoot, sitting cross-legged on the cement floor. Her teeth are stained deep maroon thanks to a lifelong addiction to chewing betel nut. She prepares her fix as we talk, from a kit kept close at hand, in an open metal pot pulled from beneath the family altar. Cutting the nut with the attention of any addict, she slathers a green leaf with its meat and sticks it between teeth and jaw. When she is done sucking and chewing the wrapping she abandons it, then picks casually at her teeth with a toothpick. Though unsightly at first, it is apparently healthy for her teeth. Though stained, she has them all. It is a habit of her generation; few of the younger women we meet have taken it up.

Cua pulls off his hat to show us his shiny black hair. "See I am young," he shouts, pointing at my silvering locks. "And plus, I still have all my teeth!" Which would be a stretch in any language. The bottom row is a picket fence of five long, widely separated teeth, the top row just a trio, each sticking out nearly perpendicular to his face.

Above the family altar (requisite in every Vietnamese home, used for daily prayers and celebrations of annual death anniversaries) delicate red-and-yellow paper mobiles blow in the sea breeze. A black-and-white photo of the couple on their marriage day hangs next to certificates from the government thanking each of them for their efforts during the war. In the next room, above a child's bed, posters of European soccer stars (Baggio, Zidane, Ronaldo) are pinned to the wall.

He offers us small teacups filled to the brim with rice wine and pulls a plastic cap off a new, store-bought bottle. Sweet, like vermouth, he throws back cup after cup and talks more and more excitedly. He confirms the history of the town's name. "Because we kicked the French, then the Americans!" He is smiling, nearly shouting. As his voice grows louder his elegant, smallish wife whacks him on the arm, telling him, "Tone it down, these are our guests." She's afraid he'll insult us with his talk of "kicking the Americans." We assure them we are not offended.

"I don't get a chance to express myself very often," he argues. "I want them to hear."

In an effort to stop the flow of supplies and men moving by junks along the Ho Chi Minh Sea Trail, the Americans started Operation Sea Dragon in 1966, focused on these very waters. By 1967 the campaign had succeeded but the North Vietnamese simply switched to sending supplies by the land-based Ho Chi Minh Trail instead.

"We were bombed here during the war and hid in caves. It made it very difficult to fish!" He remembers the first bombing—April 1967—and the fact that two American planes were shot down "five miles from where we sit." He says the only Americans he's ever seen before us were those two pilots. One was captured, the other shot when a gesture of "putting his hands up" was misunderstood as reaching for a weapon.

Cua's brother barges into the house. He appears drunk, though it's not yet noon yet. He had a son who joined the army at eighteen and was killed when he was twenty, he tells us. "He was killed near the Laos border," he says. "My one wish is that I could bring him here, for a proper burial. But I can't afford it."

They are very curious about Ngan—the old woman touching her arm and shoulder, patting her on the back—wanting to know where in the south she's from. When she says she left the country in 1975, nothing more has to be said or asked. They know her story. Or what they need to know. Yet they bear no animosity toward Ngan who they quickly identify as a southerner.

"We are all one people today," the old man says, pouring more drinks.

The doctor sits on the floor next to me, pouring tea, alternating cigarettes with long drags off a bong-like tobacco water pipe. He seems to be paid for his services with cigarettes and wine and doesn't stint on either. The old man unwraps the bundle handed him by the doctor and his wife dumps one of the packages into boiling water. Once cooled he slurps it down from a big bowl in one big gulp. Rubbing his kidneys he pronounces himself "improved."

With that, he stands to retire, exuberantly kissing me twice on each cheek as we back out the door. Clouds and midday wine dim the noon light.

*Sharing tea is a daily ritual across
Vietnam.*

We make it just a few houses down the crushed-gravel walk before
being waved into another home. A crowd gathers outside the open windows, gawking at these strange visitors. We are introduced to another
patient, who happens to be the town's police chief and local Communist

Party representative. Tall, sixty-two, a green pith helmet covering dark black hair and shadowing a cylindrical scar on one cheek, he does not greet us with quite as much friendliness as our last hosts. He and his wife own a small shop that at night turns into a karaoke bar; they also are Toan's landlords while he is in Victory. As introductions are made, the room fills; several men in their thirties eye us suspiciously, the first such looks I've felt since arriving in the north.

He tells us he's never met an American. During the war he was a fisherman; in 1964 an American plane bombed the boat he was working on, killing three of the twenty-one crewmen. He takes off his shoe and shows a badly deformed foot, injured, he said, during that explosion. With his wife, who sits at his side in a polyester, flowered pantsuit, they had four sons. None were killed during the war, very unusual for this village. I study the walls as he talks. A calendar from 1999 is the lone hanging ornament on the wall behind him; another, from 2000, decorates a side wall, this with a photo from a California suburb, a red sports car parked in front of a town house. Framed certificates thank both him and his wife for their efforts during the war.

Maybe it's the rice wine, but this guy's stories are putting me to sleep. He's telling how the wife of one of his sons was killed in a fishing accident. Somehow she'd been stabbed, but it's not clear if by man or fish. We don't press and quickly maneuver our way out of the room and back to the rocky beach.

It is dusk as we paddle out of town. A fire glows beneath a bamboo boat being made on shore. The sound of a tinny radio floats across the calm strait. We pass four fishing boats tied together, cook fires burning on the floor and the fishermen—men, women, children, an old, blind grandmother—listen to a soccer match, shouting out loudly to each other at each near goal.

Two days south of Victory we paddle into the fishing port of Cat Ba—the largest island in Ha Long Bay—accompanying a widening stream of fishing boats. It is dusk on a Saturday night, quitting time, but the crowd hustling toward port surprises me.

As we close in on the fringe of the harbor, where five thousand live aboard boats, Ngan's face takes on a look of horror, as she mouths, "Oh . . . my . . . God!"

It's like a scene out of *Waterworld* crossed with *Escape from New York*. Scratchy rock music blares, fireworks explode, smoke mixes with mist. Fast-moving speedboats zoom in and out nearly splitting us in two. We are cruised by a couple punks in a stripped-down metal skiff circling round and round, seeing just how close they can come, a wild look in their eyes. Flames flare from the on-deck kitchen cook stoves of a thousand boats. A navy patrol pulls up alongside us, siren bleating, machine guns unsheathed, spotlights rotating. As the darkness extends, boats continue to arrive from the sea, all headed into the maelstrom of noise, and the smell of diesel exhaust mixed with the overpowering aroma of garbage and fish sauce. The water in the bay is filthy, thanks to its being home to several thousand people. As daylight's last glimmer flickers the scene grows more ominous.

We have arrived in Cat Ba at a bizarre/fortuitous time. The next day the town will celebrate the forty-second anniversary of Ho Chi Minh's visit. He had come—April 1, 1959—to give his blessing to the fishing port, its industriousness, and to encourage the people to protect Vietnam's shores from the enemy, then the French. Each year it is the biggest fest of the year, outside of Tet, celebrated by speeches, traditional music, and floats and costumes in the town's main square.

The next morning as we paddle toward shore we hitch a ride aboard a rusty icemaker cruising the port like some kind of floating Good Humor Man.

Nothing in this place—not fish, rice wine, politics, even Uncle Ho—is more important than ice. The boat's owner, Hoai, offers more sweet rice wine as his iceboat cruises the alleyways looking for customers, ranging from small family fishing boats to big commercial squid boats that buy seven tons of crushed ice at a time.

A half dozen workers hoist seventy-pound blocks of ice from the hold and onto the deck, where they are snagged with metal claw hooks by a pair of muscled strong boys—flat-nosed, giant-biceped twenty-year-olds wearing matching yellow "PlayGuy" T-shirts and rip-off flip flops. They take turns lifting blocks over their heads and feeding them into a grinder that leads to an aluminum chute that directs the crudely crushed ice into proffered wicker baskets or directly into the hold of the bigger boats. The grinder is run by an engine attached to the boat's roof, jump-started by a hand crank and stoked with ice chips while running to keep from overheating. Its incredible shaking and racket make conversation difficult.

Hoai shouts his life story over the cacophony. It ends, after a fashion, with his graduation from Hanoi's prestigious Ho Chi Minh College in 1991 with a much desired economics degree. The very next year he made his first attempt to escape his homeland.

In the mid-eighties, thanks to a combination of the high cost of war and corruption, failed cooperatives, embargoes, drought, and the end of the Cold War, the country plunged into abject, abject poverty, which mostly continues today. Into the early nineties anyone with access to a boat—or money to afford a place on one—tried to flee Vietnam.

Between 1980 and 1985 thousands of refugees fled Vietnam; the Communist government was still rounding up whomever it perceived as its enemies and putting them into reeducation camps, or worse. Desperate and unprepared, many of these "boat people" were kidnapped, killed, mutilated, raped . . . or caught and returned, and charged heavy fines. Many of them tried to escape two, three, four times.

Many were caught by the Vietnamese navy (motivated by a cut of any fine levied). Some got away. The rest—like Hoai—ended up in giant refugee camps on the outskirts of Hong Kong, where they lingered for a year, two, three, or four. After two years behind barbed wire, Hoai applied to return to Vietnam. He paid a fine, and now owns his own business, which earns him two dollars a day, on a good day.

He is forty years old, but feels it's too late to change his life. His hope is for his family, his two young children. He admires Americans, he says, for their kindness and intelligence. We ask if he doesn't see any irony in being so complimentary and respectful about a nation that not so long ago attempted to bomb his homeland to kingdom come, killing 3 million of his brethren along the way.

"That was not about the people," he explains. "That was about governments. I know the people of America are very good. They love their families just like the Vietnamese families do. I cannot hold you responsible for what your government did." He refuses to talk about his own government and doesn't want us to photograph him, or video his college identification card, for fear of retribution if his image—or words—are reported.

It's not the first time we've run into a reluctance to be quoted, or filmed. Along with Escape, the two most repetitive themes we're picking up on are Oppression and Forgiveness. Yet despite their dire straits, we hear not one word of animosity toward us as Americans. It would be easy for them to be bitter, understandable, actually, even expected.

Paddling away from Hoai, the raucous festival celebrating Ho's visit is heating up on shore. I'm curious about Ngan's take on the leader still revered here in the north. Given that members of her family had been killed, jailed, and reeducated during and after the war he fomented, she is not a big fan of the man, or in agreement with the followers who still revere him.

"After 1975 everyone in the country was demanded to hang a picture of Uncle Ho in his or her house," she remembers.

"When I came to visit my grandparents in 1992, in their small village an hour and a half outside of Saigon, we went to a café where the owner was a friend. He had replaced the required photo of Uncle Ho with a poster of an American rock star. Apparently it was quite popular to do in their neighborhood. But it was quite a shock when I looked up expecting to see Ho Chi Minh and instead there was Jon Bon Jovi."

Spirits, and spirituality, are everywhere on Ha Long Bay, evident in nearly every home in Vietnam. Early one morning I leave the rest behind and go for a small solo paddle around a pair of tall islands. On one I spy an elaborate fishermen's temple built on a small sand beach above the tide line and pull ashore.

Two big concrete elephants guard the entrance to the elaborate cement building. The male elephant (white) represents longevity, the female (pink) wealth. The facade of the small, pale yellow building is decorated with elaborate wooden scrolls, its roof of red tile. On each side of the tall wooden doors are cranes made from small pieces of turquoise tile, standing atop turtles glued to the wall, another sign for longevity. Every month—on the first and fifteenth of the lunar month—nearby fishermen come here to give thanks and ask protection while they are on the seas.

I swing open the wooden doors, which are never locked. Inside is an elaborate altar, laden with bowls filled with fruit and joss sticks and small cups for rice wine. A trio of Buddhas guards the place, from inside glass cases. On a white board mounted on the wall is a handwritten list of who has given money to help build and maintain the temple.

The decor is a blend of the fantastic and the ordinary. On each side of the altar is a basket filled with elegantly carved burgundy and gold embossed paddles. A small cylindrical pot filled with small swords sits alongside. But in the back of the cement-floored room is a table covered with worn ceramic plates and bowls, which the fishermen use when they visit. Outside in a shaded side yard is a short table and

benches covered with blue-and-white ceramic tile, next to a small yellow oven where prayer papers are burned before the fishermen venture onto the sea.

Fishing is the primary occupation of a floating village's residents.

This place is less about asking for specific protection though, and more about praying for wealth and a long life.

As I'm about to paddle off, a handsome man with silvering hair arrives in a bamboo boat. Though we can't communicate with words, we sit near to one another in the shade of the trees for half an hour before he indicates he's off to fish. I make the appropriate hand motions to ask if I can join him, and then quickly paddle ten minutes away—and back, accompanied by Ngan.

We join him in his simple, single-mast boat with the requisite two-cylinder engine and head out onto the sea. His specialty is black jelly-fish—sold as aphrodisiacs in China—and to find them we must go two miles out. It's difficult fishing on gray, rolling seas. He is an example of how the free market economy is not quite working for everyone in Vietnam. While the jellyfish sell for several hundred dollars in China, he must sell to a middleman for just two or three dollars. The rest ends up in the hands of a variety of middlemen, with the government taking its share in taxes and duties. If he were able to profit more, keep twenty dollars per jellyfish for example, he'd be able to buy a better boat, maybe employ a helper, and thus improve his own life and another's. He admits that probably won't happen in his lifetime.

He lives in a small floating fishing village, with one of his twenty-two siblings. He tells a complicated story of a mix-up at the hospital when he was born, giving him two birth families—one with eleven kids, the other with twelve—now requiring him to contribute part of his earnings to two sets of parents. He also has a story of escape. He was nineteen the first time he tried to flee. Twice he was caught and returned, beaten, his life savings taken by the government.

Two miles and an hour from shore we are joined by another boat carrying one of his brothers and several friends, also fishing but with no luck. Given the luxury of the calm-if-gray day and in no hurry to return to shore, they tie off and share a few jokes, and a few subtle resentments, about the government in Hanoi, sentiments outsiders rarely hear spoken on shore.

Ngan suggests that in order for them to get better prices for their fish maybe they should form something like a cooperative, though that is regarded a "dirty" word in Vietnam.

"We should, you're right," says the brother. "But maybe call it an association. Or a Jellyfish Club."

Being on the gray sea, away from land and our travel mates, elicits an emotional story from Ngan, one I'd not yet heard, about an uncle who died during his own attempt at escape.

"It was my Uncle Vung, who had a difficult time living in Vietnam after he was released from reeducation camp several years after the end of the war. Even then, the authorities harassed him such that he had to feign madness just to escape their abuse. It got so bad that finally, disheartened, one day in the early 1980s he simply said 'I'm leaving.'

"Like so many others, he attempted to leave by boat. In the end, he would try three different times. The plan was that when he safely arrived in a refugee camp, in Hong Kong or wherever, he would send word by telegram using a code word—love letter—to tell us he was safe. Then he would join my mother, his sister, in the U.S. Unfortunately that telegram never arrived. To this day, my grandmother—his mother—still hopes one day he'll walk into her house and surprise her.

"That was sixteen years ago . . . but now, out here, today it's impossible for me to be on these waters and not think about what he must have experienced when he set out by small boat from the shore."

Her arms wrapped around the base of the fishing boat's mast, she stares out to sea, tears flooding her eyes. "I hope he rests in peace knowing that his family is very well, doing very well."

When we first met I had asked Ngan if being back on the South China Sea would bring back memories, either good or bad. At the time she was uncertain. Now that we are out here, this landscape and horizon seem to be unlocking memories that have been carefully guarded for more than twenty years.

"When we were on the boat heading for Cebic Bay in the Philippines I was so sick I thought I was going to die. I remember an older woman on the boat wearing a red-and-white checked dress, who did die. And they simply threw her overboard. I remember thinking, 'Oh my god, is that going to happen to me?'

"I kept tugging at my mother and asking her if they were going to throw me overboard because I was sick. My mother kept saying, 'It's not going to happen to you . . . . It's not going to happen to you . . . . You'll get well.'

"I also remember having put a bag of instant noodles in my bag when we were still on land, and how my mother used that bag once we arrived in the Philippines to feed our family and two others. We didn't have any money, the dong we had carried with us was useless, so my mother had to sell the little jewelry she'd carried with her to buy us food and drinks. How small is the world? Ten years later my sister would marry one of the children of one of those families, uniting us all again.

"When we fled my mother was hesitant to leave everything behind. She was in total denial that we would never be back. She prepared a box with all of her photos, journals, and diaries but ultimately it was left behind, everything was left behind but the children.

"She assumed everything was lost, even that box, destroyed. I remember her crying almost every night for the first four years after we left Vietnam, mostly because she was the eldest of twelve and had no idea of how her family still in Vietnam had fared under the new regime. She didn't know if they'd been sent to reeducation camps or killed. She lived the rest of her life very worried. My father came from a big family too; he was the oldest of nine children. Until 1979—four years after we left—we had no news from them, nor did they know where or how we were.

"During the first few years we were in the States my parents hesitated to write or try and communicate with family back in Vietnam, for fear of jeopardizing them. Plus, the new government had changed all the street addresses, and we weren't sure where anyone was living.

"Only much later did we find out that my grandparents had been told by government officials that my father's helicopter had crashed into the ocean, killing him and his whole family. While they tried to believe it was not true, that we were still okay, they had no proof. They mourned us for four years ... until the Red Cross carried a letter to them from my father, explaining that we were in New Orleans and that we were okay.

"I remember getting dressed up to have a photo taken to include in the letter; I would have been seven years old by then.

"It wasn't until 1991 that my father was able to talk with his mother. She won a small lottery and spent it all calling her son in the U.S. The connection was made, they said hello and then the money ran out and they were cut off.

"In 1992 when I came back for the first time I asked my grandparents and my aunties to describe how they felt when they first saw pictures of us after all those years of assuming we'd been buried at sea. They cried with joy. At that time they regained their belief in God, because this felt like a miracle.

"The tragedy was that my mother didn't live to return to Vietnam, to reconnect with her family. She died of cancer when she was forty-four, possibly from being exposed to Agent Orange.

"During my first visit back, three years after my mother died, my grandmother presented me with a box. It was my mother's photos and journals, which she had somehow managed to rescue and save. To me, it was like a lost treasure. I could see my mother again, during the different times of her life. Playing as a six-year-old, again when she was nine, playing a guitar when she was a young woman. Pictures of her I had never seen.

"My mother was an amazing woman. Still this day, when I walk through the markets in the town in the Mekong Delta where she lived, old friends call out to me, recognizing her in me, wondering if I am Dieu's daughter. 'You are so much like her,' they'll say, 'the way you look, your mannerisms.' They'll pull me aside and say, 'Listen I have a story to share with you.' They still keep memories of my mother alive by sharing stories of her from different phases of her life.

"That's one reason I'm so drawn to Vietnam, always so eager to return. Since that first visit in 1992 I've made twenty trips back, in varying capacities, for work, personal reasons, academic, any reason at all actually. I want to know the bits and pieces of my mother's life, my father's life, and my family's history. To know that I didn't just fall out of the sky—because when I was growing up I never saw pictures of myself as a baby, all of those were lost until I returned. It was the most amazing feeling to see a picture of my mother breastfeeding me or to see a picture of, you know, Ngan as a six-month or year-old baby.

"But until now I've always come back to Vietnam by airplane, or driven in from Cambodia or Laos. Seeing Vietnam this way, from its coastline, is really quite different.

"Despite that I didn't grow up here, I don't feel I can see Vietnam as an outsider. Somehow I feel that I connect with these people we are meeting as an insider. Yet there is a distance between us. Of course they ask where I'm from, and it's almost as if they know my story before I can tell them. To come back and see the country and their lives from this perspective is an incredible luxury, one most people here could never afford. So despite all the pain and loss I've experienced in Vietnam, I feel very, very lucky."

I wonder if Ngan ever feels guilty about her relative good fortune, having escaped the harsh brutalities of postwar Vietnam and growing up in relative comfort in the U.S.

"No, not at all. I've worked hard to get here. I'm happy to be able to show the world another side of Vietnam, since there are still—still—so many misperceptions. Like that Vietnam is only about war, for example. I would like to expose to others what Vietnam is today; my being here now is a way for me to try and discover that for myself.

"I'm hoping this trip will help me find out what it is exactly that constitutes being a Vietnamese, regardless of the region you're from. What is it that ties all Vietnamese together? I was born in the south, in the Mekong Delta, and grew up in the U.S. My work with UNICEF and OXFAM has allowed me to see other parts of Vietnam, which has all helped me understand the country better. But this is the first time that I've spent a consistent amount of time interacting with people on the coast, people that I haven't really encountered yet in my previous visits, rounding out my picture of Vietnam and her people.

"Right now we are in the far north, far from where I was born. But the reception that we've received here is just mind-boggling. I arrived with some preconceived notions of how people might receive me.... I thought there might be more negative reaction to me. But for the most part I haven't found any unfriendliness or hostility...at all.

"Initially I was hesitant to tell people that I am from the south. But of course my accent gives that away immediately. The second I open my mouth, it's like, 'Oh, yeah. You're from Saigon....' But what I didn't expect is the way they respond to me with such excitement. It's very, very heartening.

"Everyone wants to hear my story, mostly of how it was growing up in the U.S. Most of the people we are meeting are very rural people, who don't get much opportunity to interact with outsiders. Yet they have been *so* kind. Every single family that we have visited has shown us the greatest hospitality, even taking us to their ancestors' altar, which is the epitome of being Vietnamese. They are essentially sharing their generations with us, their families, their collected wisdom and experiences, which is done out of great respect. For us.

"Also, in every house we've been served tea, which seems like a simple thing but it is such a tradition here. I'm thrilled to see it is still being practiced...everywhere...even on this flimsy boat out on the ocean chasing jellyfish!

"To me, those are the things that constitute being Vietnamese: Knowing who you are based on knowing your ancestors and always paying homage to them, and sharing tea. Those two things are the strongest characteristics of being Vietnamese, and I'm very proud of those traditions."

The government in Hanoi, specifically the Ministry of Information and its Foreign Press Center, has commanded that we not paddle across Haiphong Harbor. When I had pressed before leaving Hanoi, they gave me a list of reasons.

"It's unsafe, whether because of pirates or getting run over by big ships," said the chief of the FPC. "There's a good chance you'll get lost. And because it is a *prohibited* area with many *military sensitivities*." We have yet to figure out exactly what kind of military secrets they are so concerned about us discovering or happening upon, but it is their ultimate card for keeping us out of certain places.

The result is that rather than continue south by sea, we must return to land and drive around Haiphong. As we say goodbye to the jellyfish fisherman and Ha Long Bay, we kayak across an industrial bay off Cam Pha. Surprisingly, we come upon a small cargo boat resting completely on its side, apparently sinking. Its orange life raft is deflated and strung up on the still-floating top deck as a sunshade for the half dozen seamen who apparently have been instructed to stay with the ship, to keep her from being cannibalized by pirates or scavengers.

The
Central Coast

· ·

★ To REACH THE CENTRAL PART of the country from Ha Long Bay we are forced to travel around the port of Haiphong in a van, our kayaks stuffed inside a rumbling, canvas-topped follow truck. The land route takes us down the dusty, bomb-scarred Highway 1A that runs nearly the length of the seventeen-hundred-mile-long country.

The cities we race through are gray, industrial, packed. The roadside is lined with *pho* (soup) shops, tire repair stations, karaoke bars, and people. Vietnam is the most crowded country in Southeast Asia; 30 percent of its population is younger than twenty-five. Their future is tempered by the reality of growing up in one of the poorest countries on the globe.

We arrive in Ninh Binh province, unload the kayaks on a dusty street near a flat river and rig them in the steaming, mid-morning heat. It's ninety degrees, humid and growing hotter by the hour. Given the heat, we reduce our gear to the minimum: pump, deck bag, life jacket, lightweight spray skirts, walkie-talkies, energy bars, and lots of water.

We paddle the kayaks amid verdant rice fields, through a lock, and onto the Ga ("Chicken") River. We pass small wooden boats rowed by women using their feet on the oars; past a man in an oblong bamboo boat smaller than he is, herding his ducks downriver, and a woman knitting a red child's sweater while simultaneously watching over a pair of giant water buffalo drinking from the river. The limestone pinnacles rising out of the green fields remind us of Ha Long Bay, though we are

A war memorial stands alongside the Ben Hai River, which divided North and South Vietnam for more than twenty years.

many miles inland. At first the two-ton water buffalo sliding skittishly into the river on muddy banks seem threatening, but they turn out to be docile, shy. An unusual sight is the tall spire of Catholic churches dotting the fields.

But the steeples are not the most impressive things on the horizon. Those would be the skeletons of four seven-ton, 120-foot-long cement boats on the shores of the Ga. Sixty workers scamper over the boats, which are in various stages of completion. The frames are constructed out of bent and hammered metal, set atop giant bamboo frames lashed together with bamboo leaves. Despite the enormity of the finished boats—traditionally known as *ferro* boats, with origins going back to France and England—virtually all of the construction is done by hand.

Strong young boys shovel sand from an anchored cement boat that has brought it from the Doi River, sucking ten thousand pounds straight off the river bottom with giant vacuums, spitting sand into its hold. It is all shoveled off the boat by hand and washed one scoop at a time by a pair of men swinging a netted seine. Their job is to filter out the biggest rocks as well as odds and ends of floating flotsam. The sand is then shoveled into round wicker baskets, which are carried on the heads of a single file line of slender boys with long sinewy arms and flat stomachs. Eyeing me, they ask how much I weigh.

"One hundred sixty five pounds."

They break out laughing.

"Three times as much as me," says one, balancing his body weight—sixty pounds—of sand on his head. The baskets are emptied into one giant pile at the stern of one of the boats in progress.

The sound of dynamiting ricochets off the cliff walls of the limestone spires climbing from the green fields—rock being blasted from quarries. Arriving at river's edge, two miles away, on the backs of mules, the rocks are pitched by hand into a cement boat, floated to the construction site, and then picked out by hand, one rock at a time. Once crushed into small pieces by hammer and sledge, the rocks are mixed with sand to make cement.

Despite their size and that they are made by hand, each boat appears to be identical; as we walk around the construction site, I don't see any sign of a plan, sketch, or mechanicals.

On the way home from market

The frame is made from rebar tied together with small pieces of wire, fine work done by a dozen women in conical hats and face masks, squatting, a tea tray with cups and thermos always within easy reach.

A team of men scampers about the skeleton of rebar and plywood as the boat grows, from the stern. Cement is poured into the frame and left to harden; in the rainy season it can take many extra days. A typical boat takes nearly six weeks to build, from start to finish, and they will build ten a year. If it's a rush job, they have been known to work twenty-five straight days without time off to complete a boat from scratch.

Cost? $9,000.

Directly across the river, sparks fly from welders constructing a similar-size boat mostly out of metal. I ask the boss of the cement boat crew—Toan—how much the metal boat will cost. "Oh, it's much more expensive, about $9,200."

Toan wears a long sleeved, turquoise-colored shirt with holes at the elbows and yellow pants worn thin at the knees. On his head is a sweat-stained pith helmet and thick black-framed safety glasses, one lens cracked, giving him an absent-minded professor look. Thirty years old, he learned the craft of cement-boat building from his father, who'd learned from his father, who'd learned from the French. They chose this location because of the proximity to all the sand and rock. He figures as an extended family they have built more than two thousand cement boats.

Is it profitable? As I ask, I'm running the numbers, as I know them in my head: $9,000 divided by forty-two days is roughly $215 per day in expenses. Materials—rocks, sand, rebar, bamboo, fuel, and food for the crew—runs about $60 a day. Which leaves $150 per day to divvy up among the fifty to sixty workers, which comes to less than $3 per day per worker. I'm not sure where Toan and his family take their profit.

As we climb around the skeleton, an older man carrying sand, dressed in pith helmet and olive green suit jacket, stands out. He smiles, as if he wants to talk. His forearms are splotched white, as if they'd been bleached or had acid thrown on them. He has the same burns on his back and torso, which he shows us. He explains he is one of many in the area who suffer the effects of contact with Agent Orange, the powerful chemical defoliant used by U.S. forces to clear the jungles of North Vietnam of potential hideouts.

Telling us that three of his five children died young from birth defects and that 130 of his friends have died from cancer-like symptoms, he asks somewhat shyly if Americans know about this lingering aftereffect of war? He says he can't find any medicine to help and his government won't help. In an odd way he seems pleased when I tell him that many American soldiers and their families have suffered from similar poisoning.

Though he is a sweet man, and seemingly sincere, I wonder if we're not being manipulated, set up. The cynic in me wonders if someone encouraged him to come talk to us, a theory reinforced when Linh asks later in the day if we'd "met the man with Agent Orange."

We are accompanied along the river by a motorized, canopied long boat carrying Linh, Lap, and two local party officials who have been drinking cold beer as we inspect the cement boats. The new guys are introduced to us as "cultural representatives," though during the course of a long, hot day they don't utter a peep about their province's history or culture, even when asked directly. All they say as we study a map of the area before jumping into our kayaks, as I point out several places I'd like to stop, is: "You don't need to go there."

It quickly is apparent the places they don't want us to stop are the several small Catholic villages along the river. For reasons we don't quite yet understand, the government in Hanoi views the Catholic Church—and its 10 million followers in Vietnam—with great suspicion, convinced some kind of rebellion might one day emerge from its ranks.

"There are good Catholics and bad Catholics," says Linh, when I ask what it is that worries them exactly. "Good ones don't say anything bad or negative about the government. They only tell the truth. Bad ones tell untruths."

"We are here to make sure you only meet people who tell the truth."

In those few short words Linh reminds us of his raison d'être.

One of his fellow truth-seekers, introduced as Mr. Minh, seems particularly fervent about his assignment. Like a replicate of Agent Smith from the *Matrix* films he wears a long-sleeved white dress shirt, black pants and shoes, dark glasses, and a black baseball cap. During the entire day he says nothing to us, planting himself on the edge of wherever we stop—he just squats and stares. Somehow I don't get the impression he is along to help us.

The main focus of the minders today is not me and my pen and notebook. Nor is it Rob, who is scurrying all over the riverbanks taking photos of the very agreeable people we meet. Instead, they seem particularly concerned with what Ngan is up to, who she is talking with, and what Peter is videoing. This is most clearly evident when we pull up onto the shore at the small village of Ken Ga and are quickly invited for tea by a family of three generations: Grandma, her teeth stained black by a lifetime of betel-nut chewing, two of her truly beautiful forty-something-year-old daughters and a slew of kids and grandkids.

Inside their humble mud-walled house, we sit on benches on either side of a simple table. The twenty-by-twenty-foot room is also the family's bedroom and two dozen people have piled onto its four beds. A crowd has gathered outside and peers inside the open door and windows to glimpse the strangers come to town. It's a zoo. We are five, plus Linh, Lap, and the two gentlemen from the Central Committee, plus the extended family, neighbors, and friends. The scene makes it a slightly-less-than-perfect place for a real conversation about life here in Kenh Ga; it's clear they are made uncomfortable by the presence of Mr. Minh, who they acknowledge but are clearly not friendly with.

They offer us tea, served next to the family altar, which is different than others we've seen in that it features several paintings of Jesus Christ rather than Buddha. This is the first Christian home we've been invited into; they do manage to tell us that the Catholic Church here is 150 years old. Rob sits on the bed taking pictures of the grandmother and one of her daughters, teasing them with out-of-context lines that I'm sure even he doesn't use seriously, like "give it to me baby, give it to me," which of course they don't understand. Despite the lack of understanding his tone and smile are enough to get them to give up what he wants—big, betel-nut-stained smiles.

On the next bed over Peter grits his teeth; the *click-click-click* resonating from the fast-moving shutter of the still camera makes an unadulterated video recording impossible. I know the questions he wants to ask this family (about the relationship between Catholicism and communism and idolatry, etc.) and know they will never get answered truthfully in this congested room, so I am happy to sit back and watch everyone watching us.

The conversation takes a less controversial turn, to the state of the twice a year subsistence rice crop, which will be ready to pick in a month and the seven-pound fish they grow in offshore cages, to be sold in Hanoi.

At 5 P.M. the family announces they are off to church for a Bible reading "competition." Linh, locking Peter and me with a steely look, says—in English—"This is not something we should ask to video."

I motion for him to follow me outside.

"Do you see what happens if all ten or twelve of us arrive in somebody's living room at the same time?" I suggest, as the crowded room empties. He gets the idea I'm not happy being tailed today. "When that happens we become the story, not them. That's not good."

Trying to keep exasperation out of my voice, I remind him, "We need calm, if possible, so that we can talk to them about their lives, their work, their future, their country."

Peter has joined us and is literally twitching to chime in.

"Yes, I can understand your point," says Linh. "But these are Catholics and we need to be sure they only say the truths to you."

"But Linh, what is it you are scared of? What can they possibly say that would be so harmful to the country or the way of life here?"

"Look, Jon, I will say it again as I told you before. There are good Catholics and bad Catholics and I just want to make sure these are good ones."

"But what are good communists like yourself so afraid of?" I retort, verging on the edge of being truly offensive.

Rather than respond, Linh changes the subject.

"Where shall we go next?" he asks.

Hungry for a break from the crowd, and to be out of the range of our watchers for a couple hours, I walk along the river's edge past the end of the village.

At the end of the line of brick-and-mud facades I sit in the shade, back against a rock, looking over the small town and the river flowing

through it. Men sit in tight circles in the shade, passing an ever present tobacco bong, old women scrub moss and algae off small fish. In a tiny rowboat mid-river a husband and wife team feed a mixture of rice to big fish in cages just below the surface of the river; the fish snap at the food, roiling the otherwise calm river. On the shore just in front of me, a trio of men build an even larger fish cage. A man-size fish cage.

They motion to me, waving me to come say hello, so I push myself up in the midday heat and walk to where they work. One is inside the cage, cinching the bamboo logs tighter together; the other two clean bamboo poles free of burrs with machetes. They wear faded army uniforms, left over from several decades worth of fighting here; Vietnam's most recent enemies came from Cambodia, which invaded in the early 1980s, and over the border from China, in the late 1980s.

Ngan is not around, so a real conversation is out of the question; hand gesturing will have to suffice. They point at my sunglasses, curious to try them on. As they model, a pretty woman in a brown pantsuit and conical straw hat pokes her head out of a hatch in the bow of their nearby fishing boat. She has a beautiful smile and in profile looks young. When she turns to face us, I can see she is much older than expected—closer to fifty than the thirty I first guessed—her skin sun-leathered, her teeth stained.

As I watch them wrestle with the fish cage I flash to one of my stored Hollywood/Vietnam images, this from *Deer Hunter*. Remember the cages that Jon Savage, Christopher Walken, and Robert De Niro are imprisoned in on the river? That is exactly what these guys are building, big cages . . . but for fish. But the cinematic reminder sends a chill up my spine. I wonder if these men—they are all the right age to have been in the fighting thirty years before—might have perfected their cage-building skills during the war.

They still have my sunglasses and are now motioning for me to take my watch off for closer inspection. After a fair amount of incomprehensible chatter and finger pointing it becomes clear they are trying to trade me the woman in the boat for my watch. I'm not sure if they are just offering sex, like some kind of riverside pimps, or something longer term. The sad part is she seems to be willingly in on the exchange. I've not yet figured out if she's a sister, wife, girlfriend, or neighbor. Smiling prettily she points with one finger to the sky and imitates airplane wings with

Almost all of the thousands of people we met along the coast liked having their picture taken.

her arms. It takes me a while to figure out her gesture: She wants me to take her on a plane. Out of here. Anywhere.

I accept an offer of tea on the porch and the men ask her to prepare it. She brings a pot of green tea and pours it as the five of us sit side by side in the quiet, cool shade. She squats between us, taking off one blue plastic shoe and sitting on it in an effort to keep her silk pants out of the dust. Taking off her straw hat she dabs at her brow with a damp towel, smiling at me, studying me carefully. They have made it clear that few Westerners visit here; none has ever stopped and had tea on the porch with them in the quiet of a hot summer afternoon. When I bid adieu, I leave my sunglasses behind.

The next day we are readying to start our day on the sea near the border of Thuah An province when Linh insists on dragging us to meet representatives of the People's Committee in its domed, center-of-town, maize-and-off-white cement office building. Red flags wave in the wind at the top of the circular brick drive; a fake waterfall pours over. We will be required to attend similar meet-and-greets in each of the fourteen provinces we pass through; some are elaborate—like this one—others simple handshakes on the beach with local party officials.

The five of us, wearing the shorts and T-shirts we were going to paddle in, are escorted into an ornate greeting room with a twenty-foot ceiling and a red carpet. Tall, formal wooden chairs line each wall, each separated by a small wooden table. Four big red ottomans divide the middle of the room. The wall at room's end is filled by a mural-size photo of an autumn setting, a narrow lane passing between yellowing trees. I think it is Vermont in October.

A trio of officials are introduced, representatives of both the Cultural and Tourism Committees. The only English-speaking person is also the only woman, who pours us each green tea after we've shaken hands and taken seats in the stiff chairs on opposing sides of the room. On the wall behind them is an enlarged map of the province, replete with electronic blinking lights—red for the cities, yellow for its commerce capitals, and blue for rivers.

Linh translates their long-winded introductions, which can be summed up as "thank-you for coming to see our fishing boats and fishing people."

After polite thank-yous and one faux pas—I overcompliment them on how good the tea is, only to have Lap lean over and explain maybe the reason it seems good is because it's Lipton, made in China—we are out the door and into the van waiting to take us back to the sea.

Linh is still bothered by my questioning of him yesterday in Ken Ga and brings it up as we cool off in the van's roaring air conditioner. After I had walked away yesterday he had apparently admonished Ngan, reminding her to "stay away" from "political" conversations. Today he tells us he is "anxious" to review the video Peter has been taking, a not-so-subtle reminder that ultimately he holds the upper hand.

I ask if he can define "political conversation." He bristles.

"Did you read the charter of the Foreign Press Center that I sent you?" he responds, obviously trying to stay cool on a very hot day.

"Your visit is about *touristic* reasons. If you ask too many political questions or get into political areas, it makes it difficult for me, difficult for the local people, and difficult for you."

"How is it difficult for us?" I ask, knowing exactly what he means. For the first time he raises the issue of censorship.

"You know it's me who is responsible for wrapping up and sealing your tapes and allowing them out of the country. I don't want there to be difficulties but I am responsible and I will have to review them carefully for any subject that is political."

I am tempted to take the conversation further, but decide to drop it. We are halfway into our six weeks together and I don't want us to live under any kind of cloud of animosity. Peter and Rob are less inclined, but I encourage them to back off. Linh's not really trying to protect any party line or ideology, I whisper, he's not any kind of true believer. He's just looking out for his own job.

Sam Son is a Vietnamese tourist town, packed during the summer months with beach-going vacationers. We have arrived in the heart of spring, when the town is very, very quiet. Arriving at dusk we must hustle up a family to get them to open their shoreside restaurant so we can eat after a long road day.

Sitting at the beachside restaurant, we watch boys playing soccer in the sand. Blue beach umbrellas slap in the breeze and young lifeguards watch over doublewide canvas chairs. A gaggle of high school girls walk by wearing matching black baseball caps, high heels, black ponytails pulled back tight. Women in long coats sweep leaves from the street with straw brooms and young boys crack open coconuts on the curb. A cardboard box goes skittering by paralleling the beach; I watch it turn the corner, still pushed by the wind, and disappear. A riderless white horse ambles down the road past us, followed by a pair of women in pink shirts, their bike racks piled high with fresh spinach, onions, and water chestnuts. As darkness falls we eat big plates of shrimp under a striped tarp, unaware of a tragedy unfolding just two hundred yards down the beach.

A spring storm is brewing, the sky turning gray and the humid night cooling fast. On the black rocks at the point jutting into the sea a pair of construction workers watch the surf crash, laughing, joking, and drinking beer from a big brown bottle. Trai and Thinh are workers on the seemingly eternal project to rebuild Highway 1A—still a ruin from years of heavy wartime bombing and annual floods—and are thrilled to be away from the dust and dirt, taking a brief respite on the very edge of the cool, mounting sea. Sitting on the edge of the rocks they kick off their flip-flops and let their feet dangle in the refreshing sea.

They never see the crashing wave, which began far out to sea, until it breaks on the rocks where they sit. Both men are pulled immediately into the frothing surf by the violent wave. Neither can swim. They are construction workers, after all, not seamen.

The quick thinking of a nearby third man saves Thinh. Pulling off his gray workpants, the savior turns them into a rescue rope and pulls the struggling man back up onto the slippery rocks.

Trai is not so lucky. He disappears within a minute, sucked out to sea.

We only learn of the drama the next morning when we happen onto Trai's twenty-one-year-old widow, wailing painfully on the rocks where her twenty-nine-year-old husband disappeared. Her life, in many ways, has been lost too. Her income provider is gone. She has no savings, no prospect for a good job. In Vietnam it is frowned upon for a widow to remarry. Ever. She has much to wail about. A funeral has been quickly arranged, despite that there is no body. Rob quickly organizes our donation—sixty dollars—which is everything we have in our pockets.

(By coincidence, the day before, a man on the beach had explained why Vietnamese fishermen never wear life jackets, most won't even carry them in their fishing boats. "We are a very superstitious people," he said. "We don't want anything the color red or orange on our boats, which is very bad luck. The only thing worse than carrying orange or red is if a fish jumps in front of you and dies, whether you are in the boat, or in the market, or on the street. Very bad things are about to happen to you if that happens.")

Atop the rocks near where her husband disappeared sits a Buddhist pagoda, where incense is burned to help protect the fishermen who go to sea from this same point. On the beach sit two dozen small bamboo-and-tar fishing boats. They look tiny compared to the pounding surf, which built through the night. I remember watching a pair of the boats fight their way out the night before, at the very time Trai would have been fighting for his life, and thinking, "I wouldn't want to be out in that stuff."

The sad, desperate scene moves us all. Ngan is most contemplative, looking at it through Vietnamese eyes. "As Buddhists we're taught to see beauty in death. Fatalism is a strong constant in our lives. It's hard for her to see now, but I'm sure within some weeks even she will be able to accept that it was just his time.

"You know I vacillate a lot between Vietnamese and American cultures and I think the big difference between being Vietnamese and American is that Vietnamese have a very strong sense of spiritualism. In Vietnam we believe that everything is connected by a spiritual world. Every action, every deed.

"Another main difference is family. In Vietnamese society the family is the focal point of any decision making. Family is all, individuals lower on the spectrum. Which is why I feel more connected to my Vietnamese side, because I'm very close to my family. All my major decisions have been made not for me but in consideration of my family and involving them in that process.

"I think Americans in general have more of a 'can do' attitude as opposed to Vietnamese who have a very fatalistic view of life.

"When my mother passed away her life and death were symbolized by butterflies.

"It started one Christmas—actually, her birthday is on Christmas Day—when my brother, sister, and I pooled our resources and bought her a gold butterfly pin.

"At the time we thought it was the most beautiful pin we'd ever seen. And when my mother saw it she just loved it. In retrospect, from an adult perspective, it was a little bit tacky. But I remember her wearing it with such pride. From then on, for us, her children, her life became associated with butterflies. I think it was all tied into the image of them wanting to be free, and her wanting us to be free, to pursue our dreams.

"When she passed away, that day there were butterflies everywhere. Today every time I go anywhere, for every major event in my life, I look for butterflies, looking to see if she is there watching out for me.

"On my first trip home to Vietnam in 1992 I had not talked about my mother and the butterfly association with anyone. But my grandmother told me a story that on the night of my arrival, my first day back in Vietnam, that she had woken up early in the morning, at four o'clock, to chew betel nuts, and saw a very large butterfly in the house. She associated that butterfly with my mother too. She said she called out to the butterfly: 'If you are my daughter, come and land on my betel nut container.'

"Sure enough, it did. She was so scared she ran from the room! And then this butterfly, this big butterfly, landed on the altar celebrating my mother's birth and stayed there for three days. After hearing that, I could never question spiritualism again, couldn't question the fact that your ancestors and everyone who's passed before you are out there keeping an eye on you.

"Do you remember the day a few days ago when we kayaked twenty miles, far out on the open sea? I was feeling confident about being that far from the shore, about having been on the water for so many hours, but trying to figure out a way to maintain my stamina. When all of a sudden a big butterfly emerged from nowhere.

"I was by myself and seeing this butterfly happily fluttering around me I had the most amazing sense of connection with my mother. It cheered me up, reinvigorated me.

"Then suddenly one of its wings caught in the water and it dropped onto the sea . . . and died. Which made me immensely sad. Since that day, I've been trying to come up with interpretations for why that might have happened, you know, the association with my mother, the notion that butterflies are free. I haven't come up with an answer yet! But see, that's where my American side kicks in, trying to rationalize everything, trying to come up with a reason."

At the big port city of Dong Hoi our day starts, as many of them have, on the edge of a booming fish market.

Each early morning the longboats return from the sea filled with fish and as they beach are rushed by the women—wives, mothers, girl-

Catch of the day

Watching the fishing fleet leave from the beach at Dong Ha

Opposite page: Women wait for the boats to return on a rainy morning.

friends, daughters—who have been patiently waiting for them. It is regarded bad luck to take a woman on a fishing boat; instead they conduct the business. Dressed in blue, pink, and clear plastic ponchos and coned hats to keep the morning rain off, some women help unload the catch into bamboo baskets and carry it higher onto the beach. There the haggling begins, as restaurant owners, supermarket managers, and housewives offer to buy the catches of the day. During the busiest seasons, fish can cost as little as three thousand dong per two pounds (about twenty cents).

Other women begin the cleaning process, squatting in the sandy muck, chattering and cutting with sharp knives, their heavy-tired bicycles leaned against a nearby post. Still others begin the repair and mending of the fine, nearly opaque fishing nets.

Meanwhile the men saunter away from the boats to nearby cafés, where they drink beer or vodka, play a round of cards, watch

bad kung fu movies on overhead televisions before wandering home. Their day begins again in eight hours, when the fleet returns to sea in late afternoon.

Despite a pending storm, a solitary fishing boat makes its way to point break, where a man bowed reverentially throws small paper prayer flags into the boiling sea. "It's because it is an 'auspicious' day according to the lunar calendar," explains Ngan.

The business of the fish market slows by mid-morning and Polly and I paddle through fast-running tide and current, fighting to get past the surf and reach the calm ocean. She leaves me behind and soon all I can see is the pointed yellow tips of her bow and stern as she crashes through ten-foot waves.

Linh has hired a twenty-five-foot wooden boat as his follow boat, which has a difficult time breaking out through the surf, gets pushed to the far shore of the channel and swamps on the sandy shore. I radio Polly, get her to come back, and we rendezvous with Ngan on the far shore. She had been in the boat with Linh, who she reports "nearly peed his pants when we got out into the surf.

"I literally thought I was going to see a puddle come down one of his pants legs."

Standing in the sand while the boat driver tries to free the big motorboat from the shore, I ask Linh if he likes being on the water. What I don't ask is, can you swim?

"Don't you have a 'phobia' about being on the sea?" he answers. "I certainly do and I'm not scared to say so. We are not fish after all.

"But I was most concerned about my briefcase," he says, "and my mobile phones. If they get wet, I will have to quit and go back to Hanoi."

Which explains another reason he's so hesitant for us to spend time on the ocean. Perfect, a watchdog for a sea kayaking exploration that is frightened of . . . the sea.

"I've never been so scared in my life," he finally admits to me as we walk down the beach. I tell him I understand, that the sea is powerful and demands great respect.

Polly and I go back onto the water and an hour later surf the kayaks to shore next to a family constructing an offshore net-fishing shack. Introducing ourselves, we are immediately struck by the fact that the father of the three adult boys has just half of his right arm. I ask if he lost it in the war.

"I wish," he says, laughing. "That would have been more heroic." He points to his house, built a hundred yards from the sea. "It happened just a couple years ago. I was digging a toilet out back when my shovel hit a land mine. I'm lucky to be alive."

Many Vietnamese men have worked on the sea all their lives.

Polly commiserates with the man's wife, who shakes her head at the story. We ask if there are lots of mines still around. "Oh sure," she says. "That path you walked through the sand to get here? We find them right along there every year. Thankfully they don't explode very often. But I'd watch your step on the way back."

Leaving the one-armed man and his family behind I paddle alone back into the now calm bay just offshore of Dong Hoi. These are my favorite moments, paddling alone, totally independent, taking my time, stopping and visiting with people in boats and fishing shacks, who waved to me from onshore. Two men raise and lower nets from the ubiquitous stilted shacks that line the shores and fill the bays; I paddle over to investigate.

The first people I meet are the wife of one of the fishermen and his two kids. As many do, they work the stilt-and-net as a family, sharing the twenty-four-hour-a-day enterprise. The base of operation is a two-by-six-foot shack built on sticks held together by metal crossbars, the whole machination wedged into the sand of the shallow bay. The roof is U-shaped, made of bamboo paneling, patched with pieces of thick cardboard and covered with a blue plastic tarp.

Tying my kayak off to one of the wooden stilts I climb up the ten-rung ladder. The interior decor is simple: A red metal thermos for tea that every boating person in Vietnam carries. A charcoal cooker to heat the nightly fish and rice. Several bottles of half-drunk rice wine. A blue-and-white ceramic pot filled with the burned ends of red joss sticks. In the sleeping loft a thin blanket covers a thin mattress. Near the open door a cheap plastic radio hums, alternating between Radio Hanoi and football matches.

Operation of the fishing net is simple. A thirty-by-forty-foot net is strung between four tall bamboo poles, one in each corner. The poles are lowered toward the sea, or raised from it, by a single rope wrapped around a turning drum in the rear of the little shack. The net is thin and yellow; when it is suspended above the water, it is one of the most beautiful things we see as we move down the coastline. A small pouch at its center opens by a drawstring, allowing access to the catch when the net is raised. A broken, moss-covered brick hangs from its center, sinking it deeper than the corners.

Duong, the father and husband, tells me he checks his net every twenty minutes. I ask how he knows when twenty minutes has gone by, given that he does not wear a watch. "It's not important. I just know. I've been doing this for twenty-five years."

Using a deft combination of feet and hands he raises the net—invisible when it is lowered below the surface—by rolling the drum with his feet and pulling with his hands on the wooden spokes, like an effective-if-rudimentary exercise machine. When the net is completely raised he takes a short loop of worn rope and ties off the drum to keep the net from drooping. Barefoot, he climbs down the ladder into his round bamboo boat and paddles twenty-five feet to the edge of the net.

As he nears its center, the four corners held high in the air by the now-raised sticks, he dons a conical hat of bamboo with an aluminum tip. The hat helps him push the net up off his head, in order to get to its center. Using a round metal hanger, he "beats" the small fish stuck on the perimeter of the net toward the center. This time around there are only four silvery fish, none bigger than his hand.

Once they have been pushed to the center he unties the pouch and slides them out onto the bottom of his boat.

"It's not high season now," explaining as he paddles back to the shack. "In the summer I get a full boat each time."

I ask if it is essential for him to go out every twenty minutes for such a small catch.

"Sometimes I can let it go one hour, sure. But you know, I like going out. To see what I've gotten."

As he climbs back up into his little shack, to take a seat on his wooden stool and again lower the net back into the sea, I wonder why he doesn't fly a national flag above his shack, like so many of his neighbors do.

"I just don't think there is any need for nationality out here," he says. "What does the government do for me? I'm just alone out here, looking out for my family and me. We make a little money, have no savings, and have just enough to eat. What exactly is the government doing for us that would encourage me to fly its colors?"

We have entered the part of Vietnam known during the last war as the demilitarized zone (DMZ) and reminders of war are now everywhere.

Particularly just off the beach at Vinh Moc, best known for the winding series of underground tunnels that were home to many northerners from 1966 to 1973. From the sea we can just make out one well-camouflaged entrance.

I take half a dozen steps down into the pitch-black tunnel and nearly turn and run back. The cheap aluminum flashlight I'd been handed before entering is barely sufficient to light up the musky cavity that drops as deep as a hundred feet below the red clay surface. Though I can still make out the pounding surf of the South China Sea, it is of no great comfort. As the height of the ceiling drops to five feet and the tunnel narrows, I keep walking.

Though we've been attempting to veer our days and our experience away from war, it is difficult to avoid here in the DMZ. We are just a few miles north of the dividing line, the seventeenth parallel. The simple fishing village we kayaked into today—Vinh Quang—was the site of one of the worst days of the war, with 345 Vietnamese killed by bombs and napalm on a single day in June 1967.

Around that time, 250 of the nearby villagers of Vinh Moc put their heads and hands together to dig this, the most elaborate series of tunnels in all of Vietnam, by hand. Offered the option of fleeing farther to the north, they had refused, preferring to stay close to home. They lived mostly underground for nearly six years.

The digging took eighteen months. There was no grand architect; half a dozen families started digging from different directions through the sticky, red laterite. In the end, there were thirteen exits, including half a dozen that emptied through heavy jungle foliage onto the sea. Each family—at its most populous, 380 men, women, and children lived here—was given a living space as big as a single mattress. Many died from disease due to the humid, dank conditions, especially children, who feared leaving the safety of the tunnels for even an afternoon. We can make out the maternity room where seventeen children were born during the two years when American B-52s bombed the town nearly daily. A school occupied one thin sliver dug into the wall, as did half a dozen freshwater wells. Cooking vents were dug deep into the soil to keep telltale smoke from escaping and alerting overhead planes. There's a meeting hall where they performed song, dance, and theater to keep

A cement-boat builder on the Ken Ga River, who told us he suffered from the effects of Agent Orange

As far out to sea as two miles, we saw fishermen in round bamboo boats that were waterproofed with tar.

Right: Hat and mask protect a vendor from the sun in a floating market on Ha Long Bay.

Opposite: A woman in Ken Ga stays cool beneath her family altar.

Following spread: The family altar in a Catholic home

A man offers to share his last watermelon with us.

Opposite: A line of sandals left behind by monks as they enter temple

Following spreads: Buddhist monks-in-training leave a temple inside Hue's Imperial City.

Teenagers herd cattle near the small river town of Ken Ga.

Below and opposite: She will deliver her fish to market by bicycle; he works the sea for black jellyfish, sold as an aphrodisiac in China.

Above and opposite: For one weekend in April, the fishing-boat residents of Cat Ba Island— some five thousand people—push their floating homes together for a raucous celebration honoring Ho Chi Minh's visit to the island in 1959.

Following spread: Making and repairing fishing nets is a full-time job all along the coast.

themselves from going completely nuts while living underground for weeks on end. And an emergency ward, long and dank, where they patched up Viet Cong soldiers.

The most harrowing sight I see, once my eyes adjust to the dark, is the very first room we pass. It's not really a room, more like a narrow slot dug into the mud called the guard's room. An armed solider sat there twenty-four hours a day, on lookout for the enemy sneaking down inside. What makes it so spooky is that I know that American and South Vietnamese soldiers had tried to sneak into this most intimate of hideouts . . . and I can't imagine a more heart-stopping assignment.

Emerging onto the beach through a narrow slit in the overgrowth is a relief, physically and emotionally. Walking over the top of the tunnel system it is hard to imagine the sophistication that lies below; similarly, it is hard to imagine from all the craters dotting the ground's surface that the bombings didn't succeed in collapsing the whole thing into itself.

Just beyond where we had entered the tunnel, we fall into conversation with a couple in their seventies who helped dig the tunnel and lived in it for most of six years. Their thirty-three-year-old son stands nearby. Handsome, wearing a flowered shirt, he was born in the underground maternity ward.

They've just walked into the yard of their simple, wooden, neatly hedged home. He carries a small basket of fish, she a rusted metal scale. Today their life has a simple rhythm; fishing and selling their modest catch in the local market. After an hour's conversation—during which he does most of the talking, animatedly, using sea-roughened hands to highlight his descriptions—I ask if they hold any animosity against the enemy that forced them to live below ground for all those years.

"I only remember the days of peace that came after," he says. Even in the places hardest hit by the war, the Vietnamese—unlike many Americans—have long ago moved past the war and onto the future, whatever it holds. Perhaps because they won, more likely because their continued poverty does not allow much time for debate or reflection.

I have one very base question for them: How did they eat during those long days in the dark. Obviously they couldn't grow rice given the almost daily bombings; I wonder if he was somehow able to get out and fish. "We didn't have to," he admits, "Every day they would drop a bomb in the sea and the shore would fill with freshly killed fish." He and his friends would slip out at night and collect basketfuls, enough to feed all the tunnel dwellers.

We are halfway down the coastline, three weeks into our six-week-long trip, when we put our kayaks onto the Ben Hai River for a symbolic paddle along the seventeenth parallel, the man-drawn border that for twenty-one years bitterly divided Vietnam in two.

A small boy and girl walk hand in hand on the rusting metal bridge that crosses the river. Beneath it, a fishing man in an army-green shirt and pith helmet trolls from a tiny wooden boat. Lush fields of rice spread for miles on either side of the river. It is an extremely idyllic vision of what was one of the most contested sites of the war, not so long ago completely denuded by napalm and fiery herbicides, then a hell on earth littered with the graves of thousands of dead soldiers.

A young girl poses for our camera on the bridge across the Ben Hai River.

On the river Ngan covers her tear-filled eyes with her hands and paddles alone toward the riverbank. I catch up and ask why she is so moved. Had she not expected this place to feel so . . . powerful?

"I think it's because I always imagined coming from the other direction, arriving here at this dividing line from the south, from my home and crossing into the north. To do it the opposite way feels very, very foreign to me.

"More important, the fact that more than 3 million people are dead because of this imaginary line. . . . When you stand here you can't help but find pity for everyone involved." She is surprised there is no altar at the site, rather than the sterile ceremonial war memorial rising on the north side of the river.

Kayaking beneath the same bridge, along the river that was once the dividing line between North and South Vietnam

Floating down the Ben Hai, I ask her more about how it feels to be here. "There are so many reminders of war, death, injuries, tragedy, everywhere around here it was hard not to get emotional.

"It's hard to explain, but just being in the south—though it is completely symbolic—I feel more familiar, more comfortable, more at home.

"I'm glad we came the way we did, arriving from the north. We've spent the past days talking with northerners, which sensitized me to how they felt about life, how they felt about the war, how they feel about their future. It made me appreciate the things we have in common as Vietnamese, rather than the differences created by this made-up line.

"It is amazing to think that this demarcation, this random line drawn along the seventeenth parallel in some high-ceilinged meeting room in Geneva, was the reason my fate was so different from that of my cousins and my aunts who were left behind in Vietnam. That line changed the course of my life and the life of so many others. I feel very grateful that my family didn't suffer the fate of so many others, the ultimate tragedy. No matter the hardships at least we were fortunate enough to escape death."

A small cadre of local party officials meets us on the far side of the bridge. This is our eighth—or is it ninth?—province and so far the representatives have ranged in age, gender, and verbalness. Some shake our hands and move on, others have joined along with Linh and followed us for a day or two. This morning we are pleasantly surprised to be introduced to a sweet young man from Quang Tri named Luan.

It turns out he studied at the same school in Hanoi as Linh (English and International Studies), but he is instantly different from the other party officials we've met, for a simple reason: He was born in the south. "My father was a teacher," he explains, "and during the war, despite that our family house was destroyed by bombs and we were forced to flee to Da Nang, we were officially neutral." He joined the party as a teen, he says, without pressure.

I am struck by the fact that three of the young Vietnamese standing beside me—Linh, Ngan, and Luan—are the same age and grew up at the same time in Vietnam, under very different circumstance. Linh's family retreated from Hanoi to an uncle's country house sixty miles outside; Luan's family home was bombed twice, forcing them to move to Da Nang; Ngan's family fled all the way to America. The war wreaked dissimilar forms of havoc on each yet united them in one way: Unlike their forefathers—who fought various battles on these lands over the past thousand years—none wants anything to do with war anymore.

"I think our perceptions of this area were all formed by our experiences or our parents' experiences," says Ngan. "We were too young to remember the details of wartime, but we each remember how we felt at the time.

"This is really a journey for me to build more bridges to my own country. That the three of us can sit and talk today about how each of us felt during that period, what our perceptions were of the other side, and what we can do to help mend and develop this country is quite phenomenal."

The next day we leave the kayaks behind, pile into a van and drive west up Highway 9 toward Laos. The border is just fifty miles from the coast at this narrow juncture; Luan joins us.

We pass jungle houses built on stilts, the first time we've glimpsed the ethnic minorities that make up less than 10 percent of Vietnamese and are among the country's very poorest. Mothers and babies sit on porches, peering out curtained windows as small blue buses race past downhill through what was the most heavily fought over part of the country. In the near distance are small hilltops with historic names: Hamburger, Rockpile, Tiger's Tooth. Twenty-five years ago they would have been completely denuded of trees by the rain of bombs that fell here every day for years, today the green has come back. It grows cooler as we climb away from the sea. The sun comes out and for the first time in two weeks we see distinct white cumulus.

Every other vehicle seems to be a timber truck loaded with four- and five-foot-diameter hardwoods. Cut in Laotian forests, they are headed toward the Vietnamese coast where they will be shipped abroad intact, or used to make shipping cases. The Vietnamese government likes to tout its own reforestation programs and laws against clear-cutting but it apparently has little hesitation in profiting from the same across the border in Laos. The result of the clear-cutting in both countries is massive erosion and flooding, which is getting worse each year.

We are headed for Khe Sanh, the former hilltop air base that is today mostly rubber trees and coffee plants. A rusting tank and propeller mark the site. A small museum houses fading photographs behind Plexiglas; rusty weapons culled from the surrounding fields lay in a pile, available to be picked up and tried out. As soon as we are out of the van, a trio of hustlers selling dog tags, shell cartridges, and tigers' teeth from shallow wooden boxes approaches us. As many as six thousand Americans were based here at the height of the war and during an intense ninety-day period in 1968 this hilltop base "received" two thousand to seven thousand kilos of bombs a day. President Lyndon Johnson once called Khe Sanh the most important piece of ground in the country; when it was lost, he was too.

We walk the red dirt under a hot sun. Shallow holes dug into the red clay are evidence that the business of selling those metal artifacts is good enough for the vendors to risk being blown up by the unexploded ordnances still buried all around. A sack that once held gas masks is pinned beneath a rock. Bombs—some still live—are visible through the tall grass, and sometimes explode without warning on the hottest days. The coffee plants at the far end of the two-mile-long runway are thin and short thanks to the thousands of gallons of diesel fuel that was dumped nearby to lighten loads and allow the heavy American planes to get off amid enemy fire.

Our monitors seem bored by the place, and for a reason: The Vietnamese have a much different patience for revisiting its most recent war than Americans do. Especially the northerners. They won and they've moved on. The people here spend very little time rehashing the particulars, debating the merits, moral or otherwise, of who shot who where and why in a war that's been over for thirty years. When you have virtually nothing—like most of the people we are meeting, especially in the north—there's little time for debating the past. (The average annual income of these hill farmers is fifty dollars.) What is important is the here and now, the future, tomorrow. Continuing to debate the rights and wrongs of the Vietnam/American War is the luxury of a more fat and sassy nation, one with far more leisure time on its hands.

A guide walks with us and stops us in the middle of the red dirt as he explains the difficulty of identifying the many bodies found in the surrounding valleys. Beyond the perimeter of the one-mile-square camp the area was rife with land mines, booby traps, and snipers, especially on the paths leading to fresh water. He shows us how Viet Cong used to turn around "spray" mines planted by the Americans, redirecting them back toward the very people who had placed them. They would throw a stone to distract the hiding soldier who would then trigger the mine and kill usually himself and a few of his buddies. The Viet Cong were the hardest to identify because they rarely carried any identification. By comparison, the Americans usually carried two dog tags—one around their neck, another in a pocket or shoe. The South Vietnam Army regulars carried as many as four, sometimes five dog tags—one around their neck, one in each pocket, one in each shoe—for the reason that they were more often sent out beyond the perimeter, thanks to their greater familiarity with the terrain and the enemy, thus they more often risked being blown into small bits.

We spend an hour in the small museum. The "guest" book filled with comments from visitors, both American and Vietnamese, particularly takes Ngan. She reads a few out loud.

"Thank you for an informative and objective tour. Thank you to the Americans and South Vietnamese for fighting for freedom. It's too bad freedom sometimes results in war. God bless all Vietnamese and everyone around the world." A response is penned next to it: *"Sorry but this kind of attitude sucks."*

"It would be nice to think that we learn from our mistakes but it appears the West will continue in its righteous cleansing that is as Fascist as Communism." An Iranian visitor calls Khe Sanh *"just another example of Americans being pigs,"* which gives our eavesdropping minders a good laugh.

"I have many memories, some good, some bad, but this book, at least some comments within, are really trash from both sides. This was a very bad scene in a very bad war. Too many died for a small piece of land that we were willing to give back anyway. Someone should ask why," from a U.S. Army Infantry captain.

"In sadness and in rage, I still don't understand it and I still don't think we've learned a thing."

"To all that served, less we forget."

"I have many memories also. This always was a beautiful country and full of wonderful people."

"Was it worth it? Now Vietnam is a Communist paradise." A response: *"Illiterate and ignorant, Vietnam is beautiful but not because of Communism."*

While Ngan continues reading, moved by the give-and-take, interpretation of, and response to recent history, Linh, Lap, and Luan pace outside the door, waiting for us to continue, ready to move on, bored with the very same history.

That night, knowing that they had only to drive the next day (no paddling, thus no observing), our monitors take up easy chairs in a small beachfront restaurant across from the government hotel where we would spend the night and began to throw back fried squid chased by rice wine. A local friend named Duong, the public relations man from the local People's Committee, has joined them. We have a beer with them at 5:30 and then go for a walk, a shower, and dinner. When Peter and I walk past again, at 9:30, they are still there, the cement patio around their table littered with clam and mussel shells and several empty bottles of rice wine.

"Join us," they shout.

A very drunk—very drunk—Duong stands up as we sit down and begins to make toasts, offering us glasses of the clear, potent wine.

Lap is telling more of his "unsafe" (adults only) stories, prefaced and concluded by his trademark "Okay, okay, okay." As we sip the wine he is explaining his "rules of he road," in regard to him and his wife. "Sometimes my body simply cannot control itself. When that happens, my wife understands. She says, if that happens, 'Just think of me, our child, and use a bodyguard.'"

Though it is pitch black out, Linh still wears his blue-mirrored sunglasses. He offers to take us to the best karaoke bar in town, to watch him sing. As enticement he launches into "Love Me Tender."

Taking his seat and cracking open a cold, just served beer he says, out of the blue, "The goal of the Communist Party now is to make people love communism. I love communism!"

I ask him if he's drunk.

"Not yet. But I hope to be soon."

I ask if his father—now sixty-six—had been in the military or government. "He was one of nine children and had three brothers in the army, so he didn't have to go. Plus, they were a rich family."

"My father's parents were very rich but not my father. He was very carefree and bad-tempered, which was why he never made—or got—any money." Linh has already told us one of his goals is to be rich. His father was a geometry teacher, his mother literature.

"So you're not following in your father's footsteps exactly?"

"No, I am a smarter man than my father. The goal of the Communist Party now is to make people love communism. I love communism." He must be drunk since he's now repeating himself.

Peter starts prodding, asking Linh about politics. Vietnam's Ninth Party Congress has just convened in Hanoi, where a new prime minister will be chosen. Apart from China, only Vietnam is attempting the acrobatic feat of creating a capitalist economy under the control of a Communist government. Given a choice, wouldn't Linh prefer a reformist candidate, someone promising change, rather than another tired old-line party hack?

His response is a classic deflect.

"I would just vote for a good leader."

"C'mon Linh, that's an escape," pushes Peter. "Wouldn't you be for someone who proposed change? Look around you, man, things here are not all that great."

"Change is good," admits Linh. "But only in the hands of a good leader."

Another round is ordered. I ask Linh if he stays in government what job he aspires to.

He doesn't hesitate.

"Friendship Ambassador to the World!!"

Hue to
China Beach

• •

★O N AN OVERCAST DAY I slide my kayak into the wide, gray Perfume River and paddle west out of Hue, toward the green jungle hills of central Vietnam. As the brightly colored plastic boat—red and yellow, the same color as the flag of Vietnam—slips beneath the city bridges heavy with early morning bicyclists, a few of the overhead passersby notice, stare, and offer tentative, smiling waves of hello.

Paddling up this river was one of the most anticipated moments of our exploration. From the romance of its name to the history of the imperial city it divides, the Perfume sparks a thousand images in my head, summing up the whole of Vietnam—love, hate, religion, civility, criminality, learning, censorship, escape, romance, beauty, peace, and war. Especially war. The last fought in this elegant city in the 1960s—hand-to-hand—rubbled thousand-year-old pagodas and turned the wide river into a morgue.

The big cities we had already passed through along our north-to-south route had been mostly sprawling, industrial, crowded, dusty. By comparison, Hue is lush, serene, especially when seen from the river. Flowering magnolias line the banks, fronting fields of coffee, beans, and rice running straight down to the river. Women wash children on the cement steps of small, well-preserved pagodas. Old men walk a paralleling dirt path, hands clasped behind their backs. I paddle up to a trio of fishermen hand-paddling tiny wooden boats; one slides back a floorboard

An elegantly dressed woman rents beach chairs for a living on a sandy stretch north of Da Nang.

to reveal a couple dozen green-and-black striped fish he'd caught on his bamboo pole.

Mid-river is clogged with anchored barges: Families, dredging sand for cement. Mom and dad, a grandparent or two, use their feet to turn wooden wheels, which crane heavily loaded buckets of sand up from the bottom. Son shovels the load into the floor of the low-riding barge, while his younger brothers and sisters play under the protection of a faded tarpaulin. When the boat is full it is motored to one of several drop points along the shoreline, where the sand is off-shoveled and carried uphill by women using poles and shoulder baskets. There it is dumped into tall piles where it is once again shoveled, into waiting trucks. Like everything in Vietnam, the work is simple, direct, backbreaking, never ending.

I pull up alongside a fifteen-foot wooden boat and grab hold of its sideboards. It appears unusually sturdy, with a metal bottom and heavy stones on its floor, for ballast, covered by thick, worn boards. I introduce myself to its occupants, Lien and Cua. She is eighty-two years old, he is eighty-seven. They have been together since he was seventeen and have lived on boats on the river ever since. His family had lived in a boat on the Perfume River for many decades before them.

Lien has skin like leather, her yellowed hair pulled back in a neat bun, an emerald green necklace shining in the daylight, and wears a matching flowered top and pants. Cua's head is shaved, also leathered, and he wears a khaki shirt (turned inside out) and khaki shorts.

They seldom go to shore, in part because Lien can no longer walk; they depend on the kindness of floating neighbors for the basics they can't get from the river. They move up and down the river, slowly, rarely staying in place for more than a day. A rope tied around a big rock is the boat's anchor. A pair of chickens roams the boat, which I assume must be a future dinner until she explains they are pets and have been aboard for more than five years.

I try to imagine all that they have seen in seventy years—seventy years!—living on this river. "What's changed most?" I ask. "Motors," is Cua's response.

Born in Hue, they had seven children, six of them born on this boat, all of whom are now dead. His last relative, a younger brother, died last year at eighty-three.

A group of children pose for the camera atop a war remnant before heading into school.

I ask if they are unusual, or if lots of people live on the river as they do. He smiles big before responding.

"We are not typical," he says.

Ngan has joined me and is quite moved by the couple. "That is the most powerful scene I've seen yet," she says to me. "To think if one of them were to die, how lost the other would be. And that there is nothing, no system, in this country for taking care of them, for getting them a little money each month or every year. Vietnam is a beautiful country, but there is no beauty in its poverty."

"Agreed," I counter, "but there is such a graciousness, gentleness in the poor here, much different from what you would encounter in the West, where I think there would be more anger, more sense of entitlement."

"That's a good word," she says, "graciousness."

"Plus," she adds, "The people here are so resourceful, so hard working. They refuse to give up."

Lien rubs the foot of one of the chickens as we talk.

"You know the best thing about these chickens?" she asks. "They don't complain!"

Five miles upriver from the center of Hue we tie our boats off at the cement steps that lead up to the four-hundred-year-old Thien Mu Pagoda. Long a center of Buddhist opposition to colonialism, in 1963 it became internationally famous when one of its monks burned himself to death in Saigon, to protest the excesses of President Diem's regime. The powder blue Austin he drove to the immolation sits proudly behind a velvet rope on the pagoda's grounds, reminding all that these monks continue to stand against repression, a sore spot for today's government. "The ultimate patriot," says Linh, transfixed by the car. Ngan remembers the biting, postimmolation comment spoken by Diem's wife: "She said it was a good place for a barbecue."

The main building is pink with a red tile roof, guarded by intricately carved dragons. Crickets compete with songbirds from tall trees hanging over the river. The gardens are scented with orchids, frangipani, and jackfruit, scattered with a flutter of white and crimson butterflies. Heads shaved, arms neatly folded, with beautiful voices and warm eyes that never quite make contact, eight saffron-robed monks leave their rubber sandals in neat order at the door as they enter the temple. Inside, they pray, walk in circles around the altar, bang gongs, and chant.

Linh had warned that this was a place we could visit but could not talk to anyone. A member of the local party has accompanied us, and voiced the same warning. We've been together for several weeks now and I don't hesitate to push them a bit. "What are you scared of?" I ask.

"Do not to be fooled by false demonstrators. In this place I must go with Peter and Rob wherever they film."

"False demonstrators?"

"Do you know foreign nationals [Viet Khieu, like Ngan] will pay people fifty thousand dong (three dollars) and get them to join a protest? Catholics organize it all. These are not spontaneous demonstrations, they are manipulated."

"And what are they demonstrating for . . . or against?"

"You know, they want many things from the government."

"Like what?"

"Different things each time. Mostly more freedom to make their own decisions, change in government.

"This is a pagoda with a reputation for making difficulties for the national government," warns Linh, "and they say untruths." Like China, nothing worries the government of Vietnam more than organized religion, fearful it will serve as a conduit for unrest and potential overthrow. A few of the monks here are not hesitant to take on the government over issues like taking care of the elderly, the poor, etcetera. Which means more than occasionally some of them end up in jail.

Lap had told me earlier in the day of a Catholic bishop who had been jailed for eight years for protesting. Recently released he had spoken out publicly soon afterward and the government threw him back in jail, after less than thirty days of freedom.

While the minders focus on Peter and his video camera, Ngan and I break our vow of silence and speak with a gray-robed monk who's lived here thirty years.

This couple has called a small boat on the Perfume River home for nearly sixty years.

He had been following us at a distance as we walked through the sprawling temple grounds; as soon as the camera, and Linh, rounds a corner, he approaches. He learned his English listening to the BBC and VOA. I ask if there's good radio in Vietnamese, knowing in advance it is all propaganda. "I know there have been two plane crashes recently," he says (one filled with workers still searching for MIAs, the other an American spy plane forced down over China's Hainan Island).

"How did this place survive intact during the war when the Citadel in Hue did not?" I wonder.

"They usually left temples alone."

"It's a beautiful garden here."

"Yes, it is several hundred years old." The conversation is a game that doesn't seem to be going anywhere and I'm not sure I understand the rules.

"It is a good life for you here?" I ask.

"All is good if you see it that way." Very Zen. He's smiling but everything about the conversation feels forced.

"He really wants to talk," whispers Ngan, "but he cannot. He is so scared." She points to my notebook and Rob's camera and explains our job to him.

"He desperately wants to tell us something, but he won't."

What, I wonder, would he say if he could? How does he imagine me helping him or his beliefs? It is not the first time we've been reminded that, real or imagined, a level of intimidation and threat still exists throughout the country.

"Vietnam takes religion very seriously," says Ngan as we continue our walk around the temple, which we've seen from north to south now. Regardless of where they come from, they thrive on faith. Even growing up in the U.S., we prayed to our family's ancestral altar each night. And each night our parents reminded us how connected we were both to our ancestors and to Vietnam and that in order to stay connected we would have to come back here one day and pray in our ancestors' burial ground.

"As Buddhists, we believe that our life today is influenced by our forefathers, our ancestors. There's like a system of credits; if your ancestors do good deeds, future generations benefit.

"Everywhere we've been in Vietnam I feel their presence and pray to them every night. To ancestors I never knew to those I did—my grandfather, my mother, my uncles. It's comforting to know that, wherever you go on this earth, if you are so connected to your roots through your ancestors, that you are sound. I know it probably sounds funny, and it's hard to explain, but it's something that gives me confidence, knowing I have these guardians looking after me."

Surprisingly, Linh lets us linger at the pagoda once the local party official has gone (it's Sunday and she wants to spend the afternoon with her young children). She would have been disappointed, if not outright angry, to have seen his somewhat lax monitoring of us at the pagoda, as we eventually did talk with a few monks, even filmed them, though not about anything remotely controversial. Linh realized the risk he was taking.

"I may need your help with a job in America if they find out," he half-jokes.

It is apparent the monks don't mind our presence, even as they change from their orange robes into brown smocks to practice kung fu in the red-dirt side yard. As they take turns, one after another kicking a bag held high overhead, Linh gets quite excited.

I ask if he practiced martial arts as a kid.

"Yes. Actually for many years. I was quite good."

It sounds like quite a boast from someone who just yesterday I observed at Khe Sanh literally run from a fly, but I trust him.

As the monks continue, their practice growing more heated, Linh begins to flex, saying to us that he wants to join their practice. He's itching to show us something, I can tell. He wants to show some kind of physical prowess; his efforts to try our kayaks have been for naught—the first time, he flipped, and the second only agreed to go in the front of the double with another Vietnamese in the back doing all the paddling.

Taking off his leather shoes he hands me both of his mobile phones, a pack of 555s, his mirrored sunglasses. He cracks his toes, quickly, one at a time.

He stands and steps a few feet from where we sit. In a smooth motion he kicks one leg high over his head, his foot brushing a large, rotund tree. Much higher than I expected. He follows with a practiced series of moves which involve throwing his arms, wriggling his hips, twisting his way down the brick sidewalk rhythmically—and surprisingly gracefully, more fluidly than I would have imagined from the squat man even his buddies refer to as "jelly belly."

"I would love to get in there with them," he says, pulling his shoes back on. I think it's dawned on him, the irony of his blending too closely with these young men he'd earlier in the day classified as "non-truth tellers."

Walking down the steps with Linh, on our way back to the river, we meet his cohort Lap, who's been helping us with ground logistics. I report on Linh's martial arts display. Lap can't stop laughing at the image of Linh as a kung fu fighter.

"That jelly belly? Maybe he does martial arts of the mouth. You know, like, 'I am with the Foreign Press Center, get out of my way,' *whoom, boom, whoom.* Or maybe like a sumo wrestler, throwing his jelly belly into another. But I cannot believe he is a kung fu man."

We stop at the edge of the pagoda, overlooking an idyllic late afternoon river scene. They are both in a relaxed mood and it feels like a good time to press them a little. Particularly about their understanding of America, what it represents and how it is—and should be—perceived here.

"You guys don't like the idea of America—or what America stands for—coming to Vietnam, do you?" I propose. For the moment, other than growing numbers of tourists, there are less hard examples of cultural Americana here than other parts of the world: Few Hollywood movies, no McDonald's restaurants, few Marlboro Lights and Levis. But, as everywhere in the world, it's coming.

"Uh, no, I like everything American," says Lap, without hesitation. "I like everything about America." His parents are small entrepreneurs in Hanoi, owning a leathermaking shop.

"I disagree," says Linh.

"Of course you do, you're with the government," Lap shoots back. They are definitely not cut from the same cloth.

Redressing his countryman with a dirty look, Linh continues, "I am happy to have Americans—and America—coming to Vietnam. But not the bad things."

"Like what?" I ask.

"Like gangsters and killers and crime, things like that."

"But don't you have gangsters here?"

He tries to change the subject, but I push, trying to provoke some talk about freedoms, which seems particularly apt, here on the edge of a place we'd been told we could not talk with the people we met. I try to explain why democracy in the U.S.—despite its obvious flaws, like the death penalty, wasteful consumerism, environmental blindness, too much

The Thien Mu Pagoda sits beside the Perfume River.

crime and prisons, racism, and more—is still fundamentally a good system. That having freedom—of choice, press, religion—is ultimately a better system than this one.

They both nod, seemingly in agreement. I firmly believe both are capitalists in communist clothing, even Linh, who gets his paycheck from the government. Other than a few top party officials, I'm convinced we haven't met a true communist since arriving in Hanoi.

One of the pagoda's monks begged us only for a conversation.

During the past half dozen years, I've visited Hue as many times and find it to be my favorite city in Vietnam. Leafy, split by the beautiful, green-gray Perfume River, home to intellectuals, philosophers, artists, and bohemians. Over the years I've fallen in with a group of men my age who have gathered every morning at a simple café on the river for more than thirty years. They sip coffee, read the newspapers, gossip about politics, sports, their wives and children, before going their separate ways.

Often they'll meet again later in the day, in a pool hall, for another coffee, a beer.

In the early morning, squeezed into those tiny plastic chairs around white plastic tables under a pair of beer umbrellas on a cement slab, we are served strong coffee by a couple operating out of a mobile stand. The *tik-tik-tik-tik* of motorized dragon boats and fishing boats going up and down the river provides a constant background hum.

They all grew up in Hue. Some are still working, some are retired, and their ranks include several professors (of history, French, literature), a musician, tour company manager, plant manager, hotel manager, translator, and pediatric doctor (who this morning is wearing a black T-shirt that reads simply "GOLF" in yellow script). One is just back from Texas, where his daughter was married. Most smoke cigarettes, brushing the growing ash off against the leg of the plastic table. They bring their own tea wrapped in newsprint and carry the day's paper rolled up under one arm. Most speak English, which they had practiced with American soldiers during the fighting here. Most remember the Tet Offensive as the most horrific month of their lives, when Viet Cong forces rushed the city in 1967, attempting to chase out the American and South Vietnamese armies. They were ultimately unsuccessful in taking over the symbolic city of the south, despite a bloody, month-long street fight. Scars from those battles can still be seen on the walls of the elegant Imperial City walls across from where we have coffee.

"We nearly starved during those weeks," remembers the musician. "It was always dangerous. In 1969 an American helicopter shot at me. It wasn't their fault, they couldn't tell the difference between someone from the north and south from several hundred feet up.

"It's a cliché, but I remember the GIs giving us chocolate. Why do you think so many of us speak English? It was from learning to get along with them."

It's just after 7 A.M. and already hot. The morning's conversation ranges from a bridge collapse in the south, which killed fifty workers, to politics. "The government is changing, becoming less conservative," says the tour company manager. "Within the next generation there will be a real opposition party. Not one attempting to tear down the existing government, but one presenting a difference of opinion on how the country should move forward. It will still be communist, but some dissent will be allowed. It's what people want."

But the subject that really has them riled is the new helmet law, which will require them to helmet up on their scooters within the next few weeks.

"I'll start riding my bicycle again and leave my moto at home."

"I agree. It's ridiculous."

"You can't see anything with a helmet on."

"Not to mention what it does to your hair!"

"Seriously, I'll never ride again if I have to wear a helmet!"

"Who thinks they can tell us what to do?"

"It's not head injuries that are killing us . . . it's arthritis!"

"It's not heart attacks, like you guys in America."

"No way I'm wearing a helmet!"

"The first policeman who tries to stop me, I'm going to run like that American football player, OG! [O.J. Simpson]. They'll have to catch me and force it onto my head!"

They are full of questions, too, for the American.

"What do you think of Bill and Hillary Clinton?"

"Why do you guys keep starting more wars?"

"Why do so many football and basketball players cover themselves with tattoos?"

I admire their camaraderie, their shared love of this beautiful city they've lived in all their lives, the pleasant routine of their lives.

"It's a peaceful life, don't you think?" says the doctor. "We don't want the stress you Americans have. We want exactly this life.

"My only hope is that the young people who are going to be behind many of the changes, once they get to be my age, mid-fifties, that they recognize the value in returning to the kind of life I have. One that is not just about work but also family. That is less stressful, more focused on spending time at home. It's what I think makes us Vietnamese different from you Americans—that we truly like taking it easy. What's the rush all about, anyway? We are not here on this earth for that long, so why must it always be about getting ahead, and not just simply getting by."

The central coast is hot—105 degrees by 10 A.M.—so our paddling days are starting at 5:30 A.M. At Thuan An, on the sea east of Hue, a crowd of kids helps push us into the lagoon.

Weirs made of tall bamboo stakes stuck in the shallow mud stretch for miles, fences built to contain seeded crabs and shrimps. The scene is beautiful in its sparseness. Men and women in small boats pull in the nets every couple hours, all day long. From my boat I watch a muscular man waist-deep in the water build a dam from sticks and mud, pushing a metal can into the muck and pulling it up with his feet.

Access is through narrow breaks in the stakes; once inside, it is nearly impossible to find our way back out through the maze. Red banners atop tall poles mark the center of many of the farms, their altars laden with sticks of incense, candles, flowers, small plates of food, offerings of small wads of dong. A fisherman standing in the shallows waves for us when he sees us struggling to find an exit and motions toward his home—a stilted shack with a rattan roof. Four small wooden fishing boats are tied at its base; they are home to twenty members of his extended family. When we paddle up they emerge from boats and all corners of the weir.

The patriarch is a blind veteran of the war. His wife, their four sons, various spouses, and a dozen small children all live on this little plot of saltwater. His sight lost just three years ago, what he remembers about American soldiers is that they ate their food from cans and "had very bad teeth." The rest of his family has never met an American. All but two of the adults are illiterate, a rarity in this highly educated country. They can only afford for two of the dozen children to go to school at any one time. Bone thin, one son has what look to be severe burns on one shoulder—Agent Orange? A couple of the infants are covered with scabs and sores. They all wear the international uniform of the poor: Cheap T-shirts with familiar names like Adidas, Chicago Bulls, and Coca-Cola.

They are as curious about us as we are about them; these are boat people and they fully appreciate our means of travel. They touch our kayaks, crank the rudders up and down, and are most impressed by our red-and-gray bilge pumps (which they need more than we do). They sit on the bow and stern, rocking the kayaks up and down in the shallows.

They have worked this crab farm for ten years; owned it the past three. It is seeded with baby crabs. They can sell a single adult for ten thousand dong—sixty cents—in the market at Hue. They work it seven months of the year, on opposite sides of typhoon season. The other five months they live on their boats closer to land, protected from storms and winds. Though they own this plot of sea, they have no real collateral, making it impossible to get a loan of even fifty or hundred dollars to buy a new boat, or lease more sea space.

The older boys take us out into the "fields" to show us how the farm works. From a narrow wooden boat a pair feed a fine net, weighted at the edge by sinkers, into the two- to -three-foot-deep water. One oars the boat in a rectangle around the thirty-by-one-hundred-meter perimeter until all of the net has disappeared below the surface; the other feeds out the net while simultaneously bailing with a rusting army helmet. In an hour two more men have joined and they walk the perimeter through the muck picking up the net and plucking out crabs, some up to a foot wide. They do this every couple hours, up to five times a day, to sell in order to barely feed the large family.

Ngan, Peter, and I are invited into their stilted shack for lunch. Crabs, of course. While we eat they stare, laughing behind their hands at our awkwardness with the shelled critters. The elder brother takes my crab from me, skillfully picks out the tender white meat from the tips of the claws, and gently puts them into my mouth.

After lunch we paddle just a mile to reach the long barrier islands that border the eastern edge of the lagoon. Narrow, sandy, and suffering annually from typhoons, rains, and floods, these islands are also home to the highest standard of living we've seen yet. "Fancy" (their word) homes are piled next to each other atop the sand dunes, two- and three-story masonry constructions painted in pastels, with smooth tile floors, balconies, electricity, televisions, VCRs, cooling fans.

The reason for the riches is simple: Boats. Actually, it's slightly more complicated. Everyone here has a boat. These big houses are here thanks to boats and good luck.

These islands are the closest spot along Vietnam's coast to China's Hainan Island. With favorable seas and wind, push off from here and twenty-four hours later you're free. During the last days of the war— and throughout the eighties and early nineties—thousands of escapes were launched from these shores.

One out of two families here has at least one relative who "made" it—to the U.S., Canada, Australia. The money these Viet Khieu have sent back, from jobs as simple as landscaping or printing, has paid for these elaborate houses. (Two billion dollars a year annually from the U.S. alone, creating one of the country's great ironies—the very people chased out have now become a potent and valued economic resource.)

All this luxury did not come without risk. Those caught—and more than half were caught—were beaten, jailed, fined, or killed.

A grandfather in short-pant pajamas invites us for tea inside his pink, two-story house with white-columned balustrade. His daughter fled to the U.S. ten years before, and is married to an American man living in Florida. She sent back $13,000 to build this house (an equivalent place in the States would probably run $250,000). While he is showing off his home, from the balcony I can see the stilted shack of the crab farmers we'd lunched with.

His only son, who tried to flee twice but was caught both times, explains that the money comes into the country as dollars and is turned into gold bars and saved until the amount needed to build a house is in hand. There's no such thing as a mortgage here, few banks. And one reason somebody is always at home in Vietnam.

I follow a sandy path climbing uphill toward the sea and stop at a blue cement house where half a dozen fishermen are sitting out the heat of the day. They range in age from twenty to seventy.

The eldest has two kids living in the U.S.; his son in New Jersey works for a lawn care company. He is waiting for a visa to visit, which should come any day. His wife is in the side yard trying to wrestle a green glass bottle into the mouth of a reluctant water buffalo. I ask what she's feeding the tied-up beast, used to cart sand from the beach. "La Vie," they laugh (the Evian of bottled Vietnamese water). The joke is, they are probably rich enough to feed their water buffalo bottled water. Truth is she's trying to get the beast to swallow water laced with vitamins, "to keep him strong."

Families fish using elegant nets hung just above the water.

One man on the porch, my age, tried to escape three times. He was caught and returned each time, costing his family three thousand dollars each time to keep him out of jail. Was it worth the risk, the expense?

"Absolutely."

Walking away through the hot sand, Linh gives me his take on the recent economy in Vietnam, why it forced so many people to risk their lives and how it has improved.

"In the 1980s, after liberation, the economy was very bad and many people tried to flee the country. Now it is better, a free market economy in a socialist system. Everything is better, for all people.

"You know, we have a saying in Vietnam, 'When a place is happy it is a good place for birds to land.'"

I look around. "But Linh, there's not a bird in sight."

He pauses, looking perplexed, searching for a reply in English to help me understand.

"Yes, but there are many dragonflies."

Sometimes the Friendship Ambassador to the World can be quite . . . esoteric.

We spied these round boats, made of bamboo and waterproofed with tar, as far as two miles off the coast.

The next morning I wake up in the sand at Lang Co, sleeping bag pulled up around my neck, and watch the morning light climb over the South China Sea. The sky changes from indigo to pale blue within half an hour.

Far down the beach, I can see human figures silhouetted by the hazy morning light. It's just after five and a small fleet of fishing boats is pushing off from the sand.

As the boats head out to sea, a handful of silhouettes grows bizarrely closer, which is confusing until I can make out a round ball going back and forth among them. School kids playing a morning soccer game up and down the beach, before classes begin. They'd come down to the beach, helped push their fathers, brothers, uncles out to sea, and were now blowing off steam before school begins at seven.

They are not used to finding people asleep on the beach and they rush at me, the first in our line of sleeping bags dug into the cold sand. Sliding in feet first they send a spray of fine beach sand over my tarp and me.

"What's your name?"

"Where you from?"

"Do you know Michael Jordan?"

One by one they work their way through us, stopping with Ngan who can actually respond to them. Then they are off, moving down the beach, soccer ball in constant motion, until turning into silhouettes again at the far end of the beach.

Out of my sleeping bag, I walk to the edge of the sea where a ten-year-old boy and his sixty-year-old grandmother walk the beach line wetted by the outgoing tide. He carries a spade, she a sturdy aluminum drinking mug. He runs along in front, digging up endless scoops of sand and throwing them up onto the beach. She follows, inspecting the tailings of sand for tiny, translucent crabs. She finds them in every second or third scoop and drops them into her cup. "They make very good soup," she explains.

They talk and laugh, sharing morning jokes as they work. He must be at school by seven and will be home at noon for her freshly made crab soup.

I watch them as they continue their morning ritual, laughing, touching hands and arms, a very intimate scene set under yet another beautiful sunrise.

By midday it's more than a hundred degrees and we are desperate to get off the sea, to find some shade to hide in. To reach the nearest trees we must cross an oceanside lagoon. In its midst we stop and talk with a family of three—mom, dad, and twelve-year-old son—standing out of their boats in the surprisingly shallow lagoon, digging mollusks off the shallow floor with small spades. We watch as they work, dumping piles of sand into the bottom of the boat to be strained. They agree it's too hot and say they'll quit in the next hour.

By late afternoon the air has cooled and the sky gone gray. After an afternoon siesta, I paddle out onto the lagoon alone. A strong wind is blowing over Hoi Van Pass, which leads up and over a five-thousand-foot oceanside peak to Da Nang. Just before five o'clock a small flotilla of motorboats and oared boats starts a procession out onto the lagoon. Pairs of young men, youthful couples, and solitary young men in round bamboo boats all head for the stilted shacks that dot the lagoon. Shift change.

They will be out all night, fishing for crabs either from the shacks or directly from their small boats. Small gas lamps anchored to the wooden seats are their nightlights as they throw out their nets and oar the boats in wide ovals, to spread them. They mark each corner with a floating gas lamp, anchored in a cut-down plastic water bottle nailed to a triangle of wood atop Styrofoam.

The scene is both mystical due to the fire light, strong wind, and dusky light, and romantic thanks to the flirtations of the young couples heading out for the night.

At noon on another sizzling hot day, we pull onto the beach near the fishing village of Duong Dong. We are just a day away from paddling into the big city of Da Nang and in some ways reluctant to leave behind the string of small towns we've been stopping at each day.

Sixty-one-year-old "Saturday" pulls his wooden dory ashore and we take shelter under a palm tree with him and he tells us how this beach town came to be. It is yet another Catholic town. "If we had our choice," says Saturday, "this village wouldn't exist." Translation: If we could have, we all would have fled, years ago.

"The village was founded in 1945 by families from the Quanh Binh province. More came in 1954, after the French left for good, so they could continue to pursue their Catholicism. Then we got another influx in 1975. During the fighting we were real revolutionaries and fought the north very hard. Afterward we were desperate to escape.

"At the height of the fleeing, in the early 1980s, it cost a person a thousand dollars or one gold bar for passage." He is taut, sinewy, muscular, wearing a mesh T-shirt and a pendant of the Virgin Mother around his neck. His conical hat is tied around his chin with a piece of purple polyester, a scrap from one of his wife's pantsuits. "If caught, the fine was either three gold bars, three thousand dollars, or three years in prison. See that man over there in the blue shorts? He tried to escape five times and spent nine years in jail."

It's growing too hot to sit outside, even in the shade, so we walk the sandy paths leading into the heart of the village. The men are in from one of their three shifts of fishing; they work on their boats, mend nets, or nap in hammocks strung on porches. Women bend over abundant gardens. This is a rich community, judging by the numbers of kittens and puppies underfoot, an obvious luxury. The other passion here appears to be fighting cocks; many porches host a cage covered with a black cloth, beneath which sleeps the pride of the patriarch. The big Catholic schoolyard is filled with kids in uniform, hard at play.

Despite the sour economy nationwide, life in Duong Dong is not so bad. They have electricity, which means lights, fans, and radios, even an occasional television. They work hard at fishing, both on the sea and nearby Lang Co Bay. The catch is sold to local restaurants, except for the squid, which is processed and shipped abroad. The biggest of the crabs are kept alive in aerated tanks and trucked to Hue and Da Nang.

Peter and I are invited into the home of another fishermen I'd met early that morning as he and his sons were pushing their boat into the sea. I sit on the cool tile floor and take tea. He is forty-nine, his wife forty-six; she is beautiful, with smooth skin and a long black ponytail but no teeth. Five of her siblings successfully escaped to the U.S., and she is insistent that I write down their names and addresses. Most of them live in Portland, Oregon. As a result of that American connection, her eldest son—currently working with his father—wears a Seiko watch and Gap jeans, sent from the States.

Honored to have a guest, the fisherman finds a small bottle of special rice wine; a seahorse floats inside the bottle. Above the door is a battery-powered clock, not working they admit, because they have no batteries. A large mural of Jesus is painted on the wall above the family's altar and Christmas lights are strung. An out-of-date calendar from a jewelry store in Da Nang advertises imitation gold jewelry.

As we talk and drink a pair of the man's lifelong friends joins us. One is also just in from his fishing boat, the other is a middleman who buys shrimp and trucks the largest back to Da Nang. His keys and a cell phone dangle from loops on his belt, the keys suggesting he owns something rare for Vietnamese: A car.

I ask if any of the three of them had ever tried to escape. They hesitate to answer, only confirming the penalty for being caught: three thousand dollars, three bars of gold, jail, a beating, maybe even death. "One difficulty was knowing exactly who in the government to pay the fine to," admits one. "It happened often that your family arranged to make the payment, paid it, and then when they went to pick up their relative the guys in charge said they never saw the money. 'Somehow,' they said, 'somehow it must have gotten into the wrong hands.' In that case, you were forced to pay twice. If you refused? Jail."

We are south of the DMZ now and the people we are meeting have lived in the south all their lives. As we've moved south we've noticed a big difference between those from the south and north. In general, the southerners seem more confident, more at ease speaking their minds, don't come off quite as beaten down. Which has something to do with economic success. Many of these families have members that successfully escaped and have sent back money. It is exactly the kind of community the government in Hanoi does not trust. Strong Catholics not afraid to speak their mind, with access to overseas money and organization.

The conversation turns to a new economic enterprise sweeping Vietnam's underground: Arranged marriages.

Apparently some Viet Khieu are now paying up to twenty thousand dollars to an outsider to come to Vietnam and marry an aunt, sister, or daughter as a way to get them out of the country. Six months after they've successfully left Vietnam, returning home to Europe, the U.S., or Australia, the couple divorces. As these fishermen tell the story, all nodding in agreement, I'm taking notes and Peter's video camera is rolling.

Which prompts one of our new friends, the one with the oft-ringing cell phone on his belt, to look us very directly in the eye.

"You understand, don't you, that you can't use video of me saying those things. About arranged marriages. Any criticism of the government. Why we wanted to escape. If you do I'll go to jail for six years.

"You guys are leaving the country soon. You'll never know what happens to us if you air that. You'll never know how they punish us." Which leads to a long-running debate we've been having among ourselves as we've traveled the length of the country, about freedom of expression in Vietnam.

"It does not exist here, is not allowed," says our friend. "Any time you are in a room with five people, even if they are people you've known all your life, you can be certain that one of them is an informant to the local police or People's Committee.

"The result is, we shy away from political talk. It's the kind of thing that can get you in serious trouble. It is not worth it."

We leave the house chastened about the harsh reality of repression here and our potential role in potentially ruining someone's life. We are nearly done with our work here and it is the coldest truth yet about what could happen to the people we've interviewed if their faces are linked with any kind of even minor criticism of the government. We have heard the same refrain up and down the country, from poor fishermen to mid-level bureaucrats: Be careful what you use of our words, our faces—because, if the government gets wind of even a small complaint made by us, you will be gone from here and you will have no idea what happens to us.

Our agreement with the government includes that we will permit them to "review" our video before it is allowed to be taken out of the country. We have no idea what they will regard as offensive, critical, or punishable. The result has been a kind of self-censorship on our part that I've never experienced before. Prior to asking anyone here a question the answer to which might come off as a criticism, I stop and think: Is the asking worth risking these people's lives? The truth is I have no idea if these people could really be jailed for voicing a criticism, but if they believe they'll be punished severely for speaking out, that's enough. The intimidation is working.

China Beach
to Hoi An

· ·

★ THE FIRST TIME I visited China Beach, I slept in a rented room just over the dunes from the beach. I was awoken at five in the morning by the hum of human voices. A lot of them. But when I looked out the window, I could see no one. Slipping on shorts I walked toward the hum, following it as it grew louder. From atop the dunes I understood why it had woken me. Already gathered on the beach was a crowd in the thousands. Swimming, exercising, standing in the shallows gossiping. Grandparents, middle-aged workers, teenagers. They were smart, getting in their beach time before work and before it got too hot.

The scene made me imagine how different it must have looked during the 1960s, when this stretch of beach hosted some of the U.S. military's biggest bases and R&R spots. What I couldn't imagine was being a soldier flown out of the jungle for a few days of downtime on this stunningly beautiful beach . . . and then being told to throw on his backpack, pick up his gun, jump on the chopper, and get back into the fight.

Since arriving in the central part of the country a week ago, the temperatures have changed dramatically. It's ninety degrees by eight in the morning, with no onshore breeze. By mid-morning it will top 105, a good day to spend offshore, paddling the twenty miles that run from Da Nang to Hoi An, our last stop.

As we ready the kayaks, sweating in the hot sand, Linh sits in the shade with an ever expanding table of uniformed military men. He's

At Dong Hoi, women wait in the rain for the daily catch.

buying them coffee, proffering cigarettes, and showing them stacks of officially stamped faxes and letters and approvals. One of the officers, red epaulets and gold buttons glaring in the sunlight, gives me a surly look when I approach. Linh attempts to make an introduction, but they are definitely not interested. They sip their coffees, oblivious to us sweltering in the heat, as if we did not exist.

The paper shuffle goes on for more than an hour, as bad as we've experienced during the entirety of the trip. To get their final approval for something—kayaking the length of the beach—that was approved months ago.

I sit at a table nearby, drinking a bottle of water, feeling anxious, overly oppressed.

When the confab finally breaks up I ask Linh, seemingly for the hundredth time, just under my breath but loud enough to be heard by anyone understanding English: "What are they so scared of? Do we really look like spies? Do they think we are going to share secrets with the world that it doesn't already possess?" I remind him that President Clinton arrived here in 2000 carrying U.S.-created satellite imagery as a gift, a means to help the country sort out horrendous floods then wracking the Mekong Delta. What kind of vital information do these guys think we are going to gain from our kayaks that the world-at-large doesn't already have in its hip pocket?

"I think what we're wrestling with here is all about territorialism and protecting their own turf. What do you think, Linh?" I'm ticked off, the two-month-long monitoring taking a toll on my sense of humor.

Still within earshot of the police, Linh goes pale, fearful they might overhear my audacities and rescind their approvals.

"We will talk about it later, okay?" he mutters.

"But don't you think that's it? That in this incredibly thick bureaucracy, nobody wants to take responsibility for saying yes to something new, something that somebody else—some faceless superior— might question. I mean, where are the military sensitivities here, other than ego?"

"I think it might be something like that," Linh admits, desirous of shutting me up.

Finally we push the kayaks into the surf.

Polly and I keep pace ahead of the others and talk over the wind about her dad. "For most of the war he was based in the Philippines. But he wanted to come here. Requested to come, actually. The irony is that once he arrived it was as if he was in charge of a 'gang that couldn't shoot straight.' Literally. Everyone on the base was required to carry a gun at all times; his guys were mostly geeks who'd never practiced. The whole time he was here he was most afraid he'd be accidentally shot by his own men."

She had shown me photographs he had taken while he was here, including many of the battleships parked just offshore, just where we are now paddling.

"He actually has lots of photos from Da Nang, not just those pictures of battleships. My favorite is of him and a buddy in a bar posed with a couple Vietnamese women. He looks so young, so strong, and so good. Despite that he hated the war, I think he really was empowered by being here. It changed him for sure."

The scene passes by without words. Past simple fishing villages, fishermen in round boats seining offshore, small commercial boats com-

Although the men do the fishing, women handle the business once the catch is in.

ing and going. At midday we surf six-foot waves onto a beach marked by palapas, and order plates of squid and Cokes. We sit in the shade on the idyllic beach for two hours, watching the waves crash onshore.

On the beach, sitting under a bamboo palapa, polishing off a second round of grilled squid, we strike up a conversation with another Westerner. A Brit living in Hanoi, married to a Vietnamese banker, Jack works for the United Nations Development Project, advising it on sustainable development. Though he looks dressed for beach holiday in flowered shirt and baggy shorts, he assures us he's working.

"The subject this week? Agent Orange.

"We're trying to identify the hot spots where the heaviest concentrations of poison still exist. Beyond that, there are two levels of impact. One is on the environment, the other on individuals. On the latter, it is very difficult to identify it as the cause of specific sicknesses. The best analogy I can give you is lung cancer. There are people who smoke all their lives and not get cancer. Or, you can never smoke and get lung cancer. There's a similarity with trying to pinpoint which people, suffering from which symptoms, are actually suffering from the effects of Agent Orange. Their maladies might come from something completely different, which is something still being studied.

"What we can identify are the traces—the hot spots—where dioxin still exists and continues to leak into the food chain. Using satellite imagery we can see where the stuff is still glowing. The Da Nang Airport just thirty miles from here is a prime example. They used to store the stuff there, transfer it from plane to warehouse and back, wash the planes out and let the water run everywhere. One result is that there are heavy traces of it everywhere, still.

"But for now, we have to keep the specific sites where we are finding those heavy traces off the record. Imagine if some Vietnamese journalist were to tell that story out of context, reporting that these hot spots exist and that government and local officials knew about it and haven't told everyone in the area about it. The reaction would understandably be, 'Why didn't you tell us about it!' Which would be followed by lawsuits and legal action, never ending fights, and then we'd never get it cleaned up. So for the moment we're working on identifying the worst sites and making a plan to clean them up." For its part, the U.S. government has promised 3 million dollars to an upcoming campaign encouraging people near those hot spots to wash their hands, cook their chickens well, and not to eat fish from certain places. "That's the first step," he says.

Jack has lived in Vietnam for more than ten years, during two different periods. He sees change coming fast. "And mostly in a good way. The country is becoming much less conservative. For example, I argue with my younger Vietnamese colleagues all the time that the whole Security Department should be demolished. Which would include the Foreign Press Center and its monitors." I had told him briefly about our 24/7 accompaniments. "Other than the losses of those jobs, what impact would that have on the country? Nothing."

We agree that too much focus on short term GDP growth and less on long-term sustainability is a common problem in developing nations like Vietnam. Here, even as the middle class slowly grows more comfortable, the poor are staying poor. "But be careful when talking about what people in Vietnam earn," he warns. "You'll hear statistics about people living on less than two hundred dollars a year. But those figures come from 'formal' reporting sources. Most people in Vietnam make money from several sources. Grandma has a shop, her son and his wife work, maybe they have a small rental property, and each may have two or three different jobs."

I ask if he sees a big split between southerners and northerners, thirty years after the end of the American War. "There are some people, often the Viet Khieu from the south, who predict—maybe even want—the country to split into two parts again, over political and economic differences. That will never happen. While Ho Chi Minh City is the big economic engine, northerners run many of the country's biggest companies even in the south. They all want the country to stay united.

"In general, the public at large knows—and is satisfied with—the fact that the government is slowly relinquishing its conservative grip on the country, including press and religious freedoms.

"In every office in Vietnam there's a big red banner hanging in the entryway that reads 'The Party, Forever.' But everyone knows—*everyone*—that is not true, that eventually there will be competitive parties and that will be a good thing."

Back on the sea, the sun grows more intense and the wind picks up, making each stroke an effort. We power through the heat and the head-on wind since this is our last day of paddling. When we turn off the sea onto the Thu Bon River that leads to Hoi An, it is with a deserved exhaustion. The trip has been physically tiring and even more mentally exhausting for all of us, and I sense everyone is ready to be off the sea, out of the kayaks, moving on to whatever small adventure comes next. While I have enjoyed every one of my travel partners and learned from each of them, I'm ready for the company of anyone else, which is common at the end of every intense expedition.

On the Thu Bon, Ngan and I paddle upriver, toward the elegant old city of Hoi An. She is feeling even more reflective than the rest of us.

"In many ways this trip has completed a circle for me," she says as we paddle along the edge of a crowded riverside fish market. "Thanks to my earlier travels in Vietnam I had lots of bits and pieces of how the country is today. But except for one summer I'd spent all my time in the south. This trip gave me access to people I'd never met before and a much more complete picture of the country, my country.

"I have really spent these six weeks trying to figure out for myself what it means to be Vietnamese. What I discovered along our route is that in almost every instance, in every single household we visited, whether a house or houseboat, on land or an island isolated, that every household, regardless of their religion, worships its ancestors. Which is so relevant to me since I so firmly believe my ancestors are watching over me every day.

"But there's something more to it. In every village we've visited I made a special effort to look carefully at the faces of men we encountered, hoping against hope to find my uncle, the one lost at sea. Each day I prayed to my ancestors to help guide me to where he might be, praying that someone would jump out of a market and say, Hello my niece! And we would have a nice big reunion . . . .

"That kind of eternal hope is the Vietnamese side of me. And I think it is that kind of eternal hope that drives the Vietnamese, that keeps them positive despite all the poverty that pushes them to keep pursuing a dream, even things that might seem impossible or unobtainable. Like escaping to a better life.

"This trip has really made be proud to be Vietnamese. I think I have been made even more proud to be a Vietnamese because everywhere we visited people were so extremely hospitable. They served us tea and rice wine, fed us crabs and fish, often in situations where the families were in complete poverty.

"And also in each home they were just so giving and also so proud to present the one prize in their household that was most important, most sacred, their family altar. It made me proud to be able to show you guys that side of Vietnam, because it's a side most visitors here never see.

"Before, when people asked I would describe myself as a woman from the south of Vietnam, as a way to differentiate myself from others in the country. What I've discovered is that despite that my circumstances were different, I'm really not that much different from all of the people in the country. My soul and my spirit are very compatible with all Vietnamese."

I wonder if it was the ghost of her ancestors, especially her missing uncle that drew her back to Vietnam this time, particularly to the coastline.

"It's definitely my mother's spirit that has pulled me back here. While both she and my father filled us with stories of their growing up in Vietnam, it was my mother who was the real talker and loved talking about her family, her experience growing up here. Unfortunately I did not always appreciate her until I was much older, until after she had died. When she died I found I had many unanswered questions about her life that I knew returning to Vietnam would help me answer. It was important for me to meet the people she grew up with, her sisters, my grandmother, and getting to know them has helped me understand better who my mother was and how we are still so linked today.

"When I look back now, even as we float on this beautiful river, I am reminded that I have a very complicated relationship with this country. I also feel like now I am getting to know it not through my parents' lens, or from reading books, but from my own experiences.

"And I am seeing a Vietnam that is evolving. For a long time the country has been under the influence of what I call the 'Four Cs': Confucianism, Colonialism, Communism, and now Capitalism, or Consumerism. What we have seen in these weeks is just how many transitions the Vietnamese people are going through right now. To me, I think now is an important time for them to focus on connecting with their roots, their ancestors, so as not to lose those connections in the changes."

Throughout our exploration I know Ngan has been wrestling with the two sides—Vietnamese and American—that have shaped her. As we pull our kayaks up to a cement pier in the center of Hoi An, I wonder whether today she is feeling more Vietnamese . . . or more American.

"That is something I think I will wrestle with all my life, coming to terms with who I am, Vietnamese or American," she says when I ask.

"In the end it's the ancestors who will help me decide."

The next morning I go for one last paddle, downriver toward the sea. My teammates have headed off on different paths. Peter to Hanoi and then to Ho Chi Minh City, where he will meet up with Ngan. Polly has flown back toward the U.S., Rob to an advertising job in Japan. It feels good to stretch out on the river, to explore at my own pace, to be responsible only for myself.

At the mouth of the river, I paddle alongside a small wooden boat and keep pace with it as I watch the fisherman just coming in set a simple triangular sail. His patched pink-and-blue sail raised, he picks up speed. The small sailboat is silhouetted against a backdrop of perfect blue sky and a handful of small fishing boats motoring for home after an early morning of work.

For me, paddling under my own speed, it is a perfect way to finish my own exploration, especially as I am paddling away from the five-hundred-year-old port town of Hoi An, a city name which translates as "the place where peace and quiet meet."

I paddle a bit harder and catch up with the sailboat. Using my hands I motion, asking his permission to hang onto his boat, to benefit from the wind. He nods okay.

His English is good and we talk as I float alongside. I ask what it is he likes most about his life here, in his boat, on the sea. What is it that makes him most happy? His reply comes quick and is simple:

"It's the freedom," he says, "the freedom."

Postscript

· ·

★ TWO DAYS LATER Peter and I sit in the outer office of the Foreign Press Center in Hanoi. Heavy velvet curtains are pulled shut, making the room still and hot. Peter is sweating profusely, not from the heat, but because Linh is in the back room "reviewing" the fifty-one videotapes we brought him early this morning. (Minus a couple of tapes we conveniently left in the camera and, unlabeled, in their boxes, tapes of conversations with people met along the way who told us about their escape attempts and—we feared—could possibly be construed by government representatives as being critical of the government.)

Forty-five minutes after we handed over the tapes, during which time Peter paced, pulled his hair, sweated, and mumbled, Linh returned, box in hand. It was heavily taped and bore a "Not to be Opened—OK to be Exported" label. He told us he had not watched one minute of the tapes.

"Just remember," he frowned, "if there's anything in there the government doesn't like, it will be my job!"

I have a photograph from that moment, of Peter accepting the taped-shut box. I had never seen him smile that big.

Acknowledgements

· ·

★ WHEN WE UNDERTOOK our kayak expedition along Vietnam's edge, mass tourism was coming but had not arrived in force, as it has today. (In 1990, there were 187,000 visitors to Vietnam, today tourism visits have grown to more than 4 million.) To the government of Vietnam's credit, and perhaps against its own better judgment, it allowed my team and me to travel in a wholly new way down its coastline. The country's sea border is one of its most secured and guarded places, for understandable reasons, and they gave us a freedom to travel as no Westerner had before, for which I am grateful. Specifically, I thank Bang Li, Ambassador to the U.S., Foreign Press Center Director Do Cong Mihn, and Foreign Press Center Deputy Director Luong Thanh Nghi. Our Elvis-loving monitor, Duong Linh, turned out to be a sizable part of our adventure, and though we often frustrated each other, I think we both learned much from each other as well.

John Tue and his Trails of Indochina company were then and are now the most knowledgeable guides to all of Southeast Asia. Bui Tan Hgoc and his Huong Hai Boat Company were instrumental to our movement through the north. For guidance to the intricacies and history of life in Vietnam I thank Maria Coffey and Dag Goering, Dida Conner, Karin Eberhardt, Ben Hogdon of the World Wildlife Fund, David Lamb and Sandy Northrop, Vanessa Ly, Sarah Pfeiffer, and Tini Tran.

War souvenirs—dog tags, spent bullets, spoons—are spread out for sale to tourists who come to the epic battle site at Khe Sanh.

My travels and reporting in Vietnam were supported by a contingent of loyal friends and financial backers at the National Geographic Society: Rebecca Martin, Expeditions Council; John Rasmus, National Geographic Adventure; Maryanne Culpepper and Margaret Burnette, National Geographic Television; Kevin Mulroy and Elizabeth Newhouse, National Geographic Books; Greg McGruder, Lectures; and Mark Nelson, National Geographic Today. I also received grants from the International Polartec Challenge, directed by Ruthann Brown, and Nigel Winser and the Royal Geographic Society.

Corporate sponsorship of my travels to Vietnam was provided by some of the best companies in the outdoor business: Mountain Hardwear, Perception Kayaks, Lotus Designs/Patagonia, Feathercraft, Black Diamond, Cascade Designs, Mountain Surf, Outdoor Research, Princeton Tec, Seals, Werner, and Suunto.

During my years of traveling in Vietnam I have always been welcomed by its people, a people as curious to hear my story as I was theirs. That willingness to accept each other as individuals, largely dismissing decades-long and often pointless disputes between governments, is something we always agreed was a good thing for everyone, usually over porcelain cups filled with tea or rice wine. All of my various travel partners deserve thanks for their disparate company and enormous patience; as do David Skolkin for pushing this book into reality; Stuart Krichevsky and Shana Cohen at the Stuart Krichevsky Literary Agency; Rob Howard for his elegant photographs; and most especially to Fiona Stewart.

Bibliography

Borton, Lady. *After Sorrow, An American Among the Vietnam,* Kodansha International, 1995.

Cao, Lan. *Monkey Bridge,* Penguin Books, 1997.

Duiker, Willliam J. *Ho Chi Minh, A Life,* Hyperion, 2000.

Elliott, Duong Van Mai. *The Sacred Willow, Four Generations in the Life of a Vietnamese Family,* Oxford University Press, 1999.

Fall, Bernard B. *Street Without Joy,* Stackpole Books, 1994.

Hayslip, Le Ly, and Jay Wurts. *Where Heaven and Earth Changed Places,* Penguin Books, 1989.

Huong, Duong Thu. *Beyond Illusions,* Hyperion, 2002.

Jamieson, Neil L. *Understanding Vietnam,* University of California Press, 1995.

Karlin, Wayne, Le Minh Khue, and Truong Vu, eds. *The Other Side of Heaven,* Curbstone Press, 1995.

Khue, Le Minh. *The Stars, The Earth, The River,* Curbstone Press, 1997.

Lamb, David. *Vietnam, Now,* Public Affairs, 2002.

Laurence, John. *The Cat From Hue,* Public Affairs, 2002.

McLeod, Mark W., and Nguyen Thi Dieu. *Culture and Customs of Vietnam*, Greenwood Press, 2001.

Morley, James W., and Masashi Nishihara, eds. *Vietnam Joins the World*, East Gate Books, 1997.

Pope, Frank. *Dragon Sea*, Harcourt Books, 2007.

Sachs, Dawn. *The House on Dream Street*, Algonquin Books, 2000.

Shillue, Edith. *Earth and Water, Encounters in Vietnam*, University of Massachusetts Press, 1997.

Summers, Harry G., Jr. *Historical Atlas of the Vietnam War*, Houghton Mifflin, 1995.

Templer, Robert. *Shadows and Wind*, Abacus, 1998.

Tucker, Spencer, ed. *The Encyclopedia of the Vietnam War*, Oxford University Press, 2000.

Wintle, Justin. *Romancing Vietnam, Inside the Boat Country*, Penguin Books, 1992.